MW00364505

THERE'S NO CARROT IN CARROT CAKE

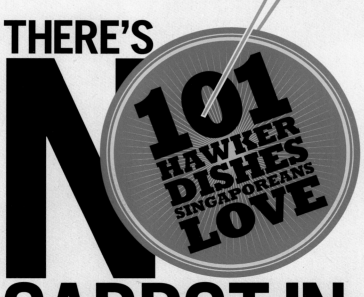

101 HAWKER DISHES SINGAPOREANS LOVE

Ruth Wan and Roger Hiew
Main Photography by Dr Leslie Tay

E

EPIGRAM BOOKS / SINGAPORE

CONTENTS

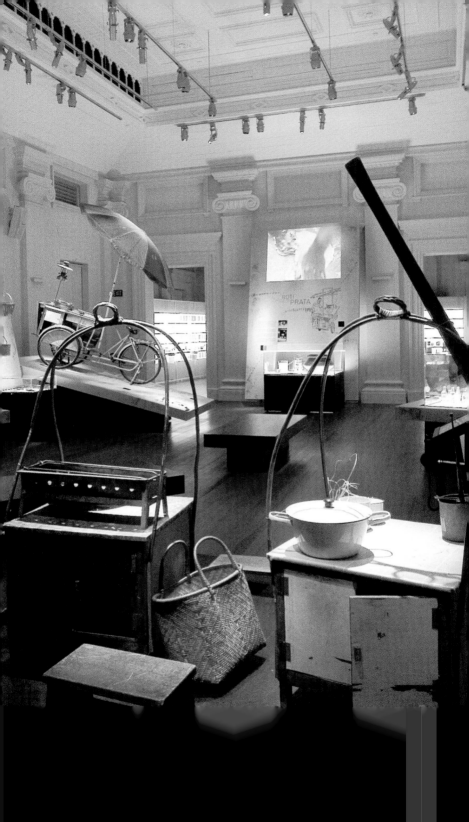

FOREWORD
BY
PROFESSOR TOMMY KOH

It is with great pleasure that I write the foreword to this book. Every foreign diplomat, visitor, expatriate and lover of food should acquire a copy of this book. There are three reasons for my enthusiasm.

First, Singapore is a very young country. We have only existed as an independent country for 45 years. We are, therefore, still in the process of forging a nation. One of the commonalities which unite and bond us as one united people is our love for our unique hawker food or street food.

All Singaporeans, irrespective of race, language, religion, love the same classic dishes. For example, for breakfast, we love to eat kaya toast with soft boiled eggs, nasi lemak and roti prata. For lunch, we love to eat chicken rice, mee siam and nasi biryani. For dinner, it is not unusual for a family to order a combination of dishes of different ethnic backgrounds, for example, satay from a Malay stall, mee goreng from an Indian stall and chilli crab from a Chinese stall, accompanied by sugarcane juice, teh tarik and soya bean milk.

I remember reading a survey of Singaporeans who live and work abroad. They were asked what they missed most about Singapore. All of them replied that they missed their family and the hawker food. I have a good friend who, upon his return, goes to the Adam

Road Hawker Centre to have his favourite nasi lemak. Another good friend heads for another venue for her favourite roti prata. A third friend hungers for laksa and char kway teow. So, my first point is that our hawker food bonds us as Singaporeans and anchors Singaporeans abroad to Singapore.

Second, the open air hawker centres and the air-conditioned food courts of Singapore are places where Singaporeans of all social classes and income groups eat together. Food is a great social leveller in Singapore. Unlike the French, who do not share their food secrets with their friends, Singaporeans love to share their culinary discoveries with their friends and online. As a result, we will find rich and poor Singaporeans queuing up and waiting patiently for their favourite hawker food.

The son of a new foreign ambassador in Singapore called on me recently. It was his first visit to Singapore. He had gone to the Food Republic food court at Wisma Atria for lunch. He told me that he was amazed. He had never seen such a variety of food or such a diverse group of diners. I told him that he had seen one of the miracles of Singapore.

Third, Singapore's hawker food is a culinary achievement which we should celebrate. In some of our hawker food, we find the fusion of different culinary traditions. For example, you will not find fish head curry or mee goreng in India. You will not find Chinese rojak or char kway teow or chilli crab or black pepper crab in China. Malay dishes, such as nasi goreng, tauhu goreng and tauhu telur, are probably the results of the fusion of different culinary traditions. Our hawker food

"Singapore's hawker food is a culinary achievement which we should celebrate."

is, therefore, an example of the success of Singapore's multi-culturalism. But, just as important, is the fact that some of our hawker dishes are magnificent culinary achievements.

I would argue that our char kway teow and laksa are better than any pasta dish in the world. I cannot think of any Western salad that can compete with our Chinese rojak. I also think that our roti prata, eaten while hot and fluffy, with chicken curry, beats any pizza I have ever eaten. Fish head curry, chilli crab, black pepper crab are simply heavenly.

Because of the importance of our hawker food to Singapore, the National Museum of Singapore has devoted one of its living galleries (see page 10) to it. And in recognition of the importance of documenting Singapore's hawker food heritage, the National Heritage Board has co-funded this book under its Heritage Industry Incentive Programme. Finally, in order to ensure the continuity of this wonderful cuisine and to raise the standard of cooking, I would appeal to the ITE (Institute of Technical Education) to consider opening a cooking school to teach aspiring chefs how to cook our hawker dishes to perfection.

Prof Tommy Koh
Chairman
National Heritage Board

LET'S GET STARTED

"Welcome to the ubiquitous world of the Singapore food court or hawker centre. The young, the old, the well-heeled and slippered – they are all here, eating and drinking like there is no tomorrow."

You enter and are immediately windsocked by what you see, smell and feel. Before you, a mass of tables and chairs, arranged in some sort of regular pattern, filled by hordes of people slurping and gulping. And, in neat lines, lighted banners invite you to explore an array of cuisines – "PIG ORGANS SOUP" yells out one such banner, while another says, rather mysteriously, "ECONOMY RICE". You cannot help but notice a few others "LOR MEE", "ROTI PRATA" and "NASI PADANG". What does it all mean?

You start walking past the stalls. There are brilliant fires under blackened woks, sudden gushes of steam as lids are lifted, and cavernous pots of curries and soups bubbling away. Your stomach is rumbling with desire and you want to order something to eat and drink. But what to order? And, how to pronounce the names of all these dishes? How to explore this alien world of Singapore street food, also commonly known as hawker food? Suddenly, a sharp feeling of intimidation begins to creep up your back.

Welcome to the ubiquitous world of the Singapore food court or hawker centre. The young, the old, the well-heeled and slippered – they are all here, eating and drinking like there is no tomorrow. While you remain positive and want to jump in and experience the depths of this culinary and sensory fiesta, while you want to "hang with the locals" and satiate your desire for the amazing cornucopia of local dishes that you have heard so much about, including a few that have "fusion" influences or have been given innovative modern twists, you also feel, well, to put it quite simply, lost.

That is when you pull out this book. Heaving a huge sigh of relief, you realise you have a secret weapon that will help you navigate through picking the right dishes, ordering them properly and eating them with local flair. Suddenly, your mood changes: you sense you will emerge triumphant, full of good humour, the prize of delicious local culinary delights in hand.

Yes. This book is meant for you – the foreigner, the expatriate, the tourist. It is for you to whip out when you are feeling helpless and hopeless, standing in front

"This book is not meant to be read from A to Z. It is a rough-and-tumble guide, a don't-leave-home-without-it accompaniment to Singapore's food courts and hawker centres."

of a banner that proclaims in red font, full caps "BUBOR CHA CHA". It is arranged alphabetically for that very moment when you find yourself smitten by the taste of Laksa and wonder what really goes into making it (and how to pronounce it correctly!) In addition, there is **The Extremely Useful Index** at the back of the book, so that whether something is called Chicken Curry, Kari Ayam, Rendang Ayam or Gulai Ayam (they're all the same thing!), you'll be able to use the index to find the right page that explains what it is, before the local standing behind you grumbles under his breath, "Hurry up la!"

This book is not meant to be read from A to Z. It is a rough-and-tumble guide, a don't-leave-home-without-it accompaniment to Singapore's food courts and hawker centres. It explains 101 hawker dishes (food, drinks and desserts) – their origins, their ingredients, how they are cooked, how they are to be eaten, and what makes them special. It corrects misconceptions – yes, there's NO carrot in carrot cake – and it also suggests food pairings – how else would you know that the perfect complement to Chicken Rice is Lime Juice or that Tiger Beer goes really well with Curry Fish Head?

10 THINGS YOU NEED TO KNOW

But wait. Before you go rushing out the door, here are the top 10 things you need to know to get the best out of your hawker food experience.

1 DRESS CODE
No one wears a suit to eat street food.

2 CHOPE!
Before ordering your food, "chope" a table, meaning reserve a table, by placing a packet of tissue paper on it. And remember, if you see an empty table with a tissue paper packet on it, it may already be reserved!

3 FOOD HYGIENIC RATING
Every stall is given a cleanliness rating – "A" is best while "C" is worst. However, some locals believe that the lower the cleanliness level, the yummier the food!

A	B	C
Excellent >85%	Good 70% – 84%	Average 50% – 69%

4 FIXED PRICES
Prices of dishes cannot be bargained with.

5 WHAT DID YOU SAY?
Singaporeans speak very fast. Hawkers are the exception. They speak exceptionally fast and their machine-gun-paced English can seem exceptionally confusing. But, no worries. The following samples will help you get into the swing of things.

"Yes what you want?", "What you want?", "Yes?" or "WHAT?" = *"Good day. How may I help you? What would you like to order?"*

"Chilli no chilli?" = *"Would you prefer your dish with hot spicy chilli or not?"*

"Hot cold?" = *"Do you wish to order the hot version or the cold version of this dish?"*

⑥ CUSTOMERS CAN CUSTOMISE

Feel free to ask the hawker to add more of certain ingredients or to omit certain non-essential ingredients to the dish. For example, for Chicken Rice, you can ask the hawker for more rice or cucumbers. You can also ask the hawker to make a dish non-spicy, or to put the chilli by the side. The exception would be curries, Chilli Crab, Laksa, and other spicy dishes, where spiciness is integral to the dish.

"Uncle, Wanton Mee. No chilli please."

⑦ TRY! TRY! TRY!

When eating with friends, it is common to try a bit of each other's dishes.

⑨ SHARE YOUR CALORIES

Some hawker dishes have to be shared – there is no such thing as an individual portion of Curry Fish Head, Chilli Crab or Black Pepper Crab.

⑧ ONE CARROT CAKE, ONE POPIAH, ONE ROJAK

It is also common to order a few dishes to share with friends – favourite dishes for sharing include Popiah, Oyster Omelette, Satay, Kueh Pie Tee, Indian Rojak and Chinese Rojak.

⑩ HALAL

When sharing dishes, ensure that dishes from a Malay or Muslim stall are eaten only with cutlery from that stall. If you are eating at a place where utensils are centralised, then this rule does not apply.

GET SET, READY, GO!

You are now ready for your hawker food experience. Go, order, eat and be satisfied!

USE THE EXTREMELY USEFUL INDEX!

If you encounter a dish you want to find out more about, look it up alphabetically in our main guide. But if it is not there, check **The Extremely Useful Index** at the back of the book, which lists all the various names by which that dish is referred to.

OODLES OF NOODLES

Know your noodles to avoid ordering wrongly or looking silly!

① BEE HOON

Thin, white and long, these noodles are made from rice flour and are also known as rice vermicelli. Bee Hoon is such a versatile noodle – it can be stir-fried and taken as a simple hot breakfast or served in healthy fish soup, (like Fish Ball Noodles). Bee Hoon can also be transformed into a spicy Malay dish called Mee Siam.

② CHOR BEE HOON

The less common Bee Hoon, Chor Bee Hoon is thicker and whiter than Bee Hoon. Freshly made, it is the preferred noodle for Sliced Fish Noodle Soup or Laksa.

③ KWAY TEOW

Flat, wide and white, these freshly made rice flour noodles are smooth and soft, with some bite. Kway Teow is most famously used to make Char Kway Teow, a dish where the flat rice noodles are blackened with sauce and stir-fried in a feisty combination of sauces and toppings. Kway Teow is also used in Beef Kway Teow, Hor Fun and Ipoh Hor Fun. In such dishes, the Kway Teow used is superlatively soft, practically melts in your mouth and slides down your throat, like silk. The Kway Teow used in Ipoh Hor Fun tends to be less wide than in the other dishes.

④ MEE

Freshly made egg noodles, Mee is thick, yellow and long. This is like the Average Joe of noodles, the most common noodle around in Singapore, versatile enough to be paired with "soup" or "dry" dishes (where soup is served on the side), like Prawn Mee and Yong Tau Foo, and even, thick gravy dishes, like Mee Rebus. Perhaps the most famous dish which uses Mee is Hokkien Mee. The Malays also use Mee to make their signature dish, Mee Goreng.

⑤ MEE TAI BAK

This noodle may win the "Noodle with the Most Interesting Shape" award, if there were such a thing. Looking like elongated rain droplets, or like short worms, Mee Tai Bak is thick, white and short. The noodles are slightly chewy, bouncy in texture and are used exclusively in Laksa.

⑥ MEE POK

Like Mee Kia, good Mee Pok is springy with bounce, and good versions are hard to find. This thin, flat, yellow noodle, similar in look to fettuccine, is often found in Bak Chor Mee.

⑦ MEE KIA

Good Mee Kia is springy, not soggy, with bounce. These noodles should not stick together too much when you handle them with your utensils. However, good Mee Kia is hard to find as most hawkers purchase factory-made Mee Kia to cook their dishes. The best hawkers will make their own Mee Kia by hand, on site. This thin, yellow and long noodle, similar in look to angel-hair spaghetti, is the staunch noodle-of-choice for Wanton Mee.

FOOD ON FOOT

Street hawkers have been feeding our nation for decades.

I tinerant food hawkers used to ply the streets of Singapore, cooking and feeding their customers in makeshift mobile carts and stalls. As Singapore moved from Third World to First, food hawkers also "upgraded" to permanent locations, known as hawker centres, the most famous of which is Lau Pa Sat. Under one roof, an amazing variety of food from all races and traditions were available to the hungry customer at often dirt-cheap prices. This tradition of hawker centres remains till today, where you can get a rice or noodle dish for $3.00 – $5.00 and a drink or dessert for $1.00 – $3.00.

Happily, food court business chain giants like Food Junction, Food Republic, Kopitiam and Koufu go to great lengths to ensure that the authenticity of the hawker food they serve is not compromised. Singaporeans who love air-conditioned comfort flock to these new places with their bright lights and fancy designs.

Yet, the true foodie will tell you that the best hawker food is still found in the dimly lit, slightly muddied halls of hawker centres of old. Places like ABC Brickworks Food Centre, Adam Road Food Centre, Fengshan Food Centre, Old Airport Road Food Centre and Chinatown Complex Market, although not air-conditioned, will provide the comforts of truly authentic and amazingly scrumptious hawker dishes, all of which are explained in loving detail in this book.

Experience Singapore's Street Food Heritage

For a truly interactive experience, hop over to the National Museum and check out the "Singapore Living Gallery: Food", one of the permanent exhibitions of the museum. There's no better way to "live" through the heydays of Singapore's street life from the 1950s to the 1970s – you will discover how Singapore street food reflects the ethnic diversity, cross-cultural exchanges and cultural innovations of Singapore. There are even mouth-watering documentaries and short films on Singapore street food classics, like Nasi Lemak, Chicken Rice, Bak Kut Teh, and video art about Laksa, Satay and Roti Prata. There's plenty of food for thought.

National Museum of Singapore
93 Stamford Road, Singapore 178897
www.nationalmuseum.sg

Singapore History Gallery: 10am – 6pm daily
Singapore Living Gallery: 10am – 8pm daily

Access to the Singapore History Gallery and all Living Galleries: adults $10.00, children (aged between 7 and 18) $5.00, free admission for senior citizens (aged 60 and above), students and full-time National Servicemen (NSFs). Terms and Conditions apply. The Living Galleries are also free to all between 6pm and 8pm daily.

鱿魚蕹菜 S3 S4 S5
uttlefish Kang Kong

包另加三角 An Additional 30 cents for Take Aw

FOOD A TO Z

Chinese

Malay/Peranakan

Indian

Fill your growling stomach with the delights of these dishes that are suitable for breakfast, lunch, dinner or simply as a snack! The alphabetised and colour-coded items (red for a Chinese dish, green for a Malay or Peranakan dish and pink for an Indian dish) will certainly help to whet your appetite, as you browse through and plan your culinary street food journey!

And remember, if you cannot find the dish in this main section, look for it in **The Extremely Useful Index** at the back of the book. Sometimes, dishes are called by different names, but the index lists all the common names for all the dishes!

ANG KU KUEH
ANG KOO KU-AY

It's gummy and yummy. Known as "red tortoise cake" in Hokkien, this sticky steamed dumpling comprises a glutinous outer covering that encloses a sweetened filling of roasted ground peanuts, bean paste or green bean paste. The outer skin is a dough made from glutinous rice flour and steamed sweet potato. Food colouring – usually red, but purple, yellow or green are also used sometimes – is added and the dough is wrapped around the filling and shaped into a big ball which is then pressed into a special mould, giving the Ang Ku Kueh its unique shape and pattern, that is similar to a tortoise's shell. The "cake" is then steamed. Ang Ku Kueh is typically served on a small piece of green banana leaf.

Ang Ku Kueh is commonly taken for breakfast or as a snack. It is also popular among the Chinese for celebrations and special occasions, due to its bright red appearance (as red is auspicious to the Chinese). In recent times, innovative hawkers have started adding new fillings to traditional Ang Ku Kueh, including durian, chicken and mushroom, and coffee.

* *You may also like Char Siew Bao, Chee Cheong Fun, Chwee Kueh, Muah Chee and Soon Kueh.*

BAK CHANG

The Egyptians erected monumental pyramids; the inventive Chinese shaped delicious Zongzi: mini pyramid-shaped rice dumplings the Hokkiens call Bak Chang.

A really good Bak Chang has grainy glutinous rice flavoured with pandan (which infuses the rice with a unique scent), shallots, garlic, coriander powder and pepper. The grains are not too mashed up and not too sticky. Chestnuts, cooked to the perfect texture, add a nutty edge. Pork chunks, mushroom and sometimes salted egg yolk complete the package. (A close cousin of Bak Chang is Nonya Chang, which is the sweeter Peranakan version.)

For best effect, savour Bak Chang with your bare hands. You can then feel the soft texture of the bamboo leaves as you unwrap the content before hungrily biting into the fragrant rice dumpling. Chinese tea lessens the oily feel so you can gobble up yet another Bak Chang!

BAK CHOR MEE
BAH CHOR MEE

If you like spaghetti bolognese, you might rave about Bak Chor Mee – one is Italian, the other addictive. Bak Chor Mee simply means minced meat noodles in Hokkien. This noodle dish is almost always served dry with a separate serving of soup on the side. The noodles – mee pok (flat yellow noodles, similar to fettuccine) or mee kia (thin yellow noodles, similar to angel-hair spaghetti) are cooked by quickly blanching them in boiling water. They are then doused in a heady mixture of black vinegar, dark soya sauce and chilli sauce, and topped with freshly cooked minced pork, pork slices, pork balls, pork liver, braised sliced mushrooms, bean sprouts and a leaf of lettuce. Crispy bits of pork lard and ti'po (dried sole fish) are added to make the faint-hearted swoon.

* You may also like Ban Mian, Fish Ball Noodles and Foochow Fish Ball Noodles.

SINGAPORE CLASSIC

BAK KUT TEH
BAH KOOT TAY

When was the last time you tackled pork ribs using chopsticks? That's what you need for this hearty soup that comprises pork ribs boiled with garlic and a mixture of spices, including cinnamon, star anise, cumin and fennel. (If your chopstick skills are not so good, don't worry – locals love to savour these ribs using their hands, so you can do it too!)

There are two versions of Bak Kut Teh in Singapore. The Hokkien version has dark soup and a herbal taste. The Teochew version has clear soup and includes a generous dose of white pepper, making the soup spicy. Bak Kut Teh is a heartwarming dish that can be taken for breakfast. Served with white rice, side dishes to order include: stewed tau pok (puffy tofu cubes), you tiao (deep-fried dough crullers) and mei cai (sweet preserved vegetables in soya sauce). Dark soya sauce to dip the meat in, together with red cut chillies, is also heavenly. In Hokkien and Teochew, "bak kut" means pork rib and "teh" means tea. Indeed, some hawkers will still provide a small metal pot of Chinese tea to accompany this fragrant soup dish.

SINGAPORE CLASSIC

5

BAN MIAN
BAHN MEE-AN

Handmade noodles cooked in soup actually tastes better than it sounds. This dish is unique because the noodles are made fresh at the hawker stall. (Other noodle stalls typically buy factory-made noodles.) Because of this, Ban Mian is considered a healthy option. White, fresh noodles, usually flat like fettuccine, in hand-torn shapes, or thin and round like spaghetti, are served in a clear soup and topped with crispy ikan bilis (dried anchovies), chicken slices, braised sliced mushrooms, minced pork and green leafy vegetables. Another unique aspect of Ban Mian is the raw egg that is cracked into the hot noodle dish just before it is served. The result is a half-cooked egg which adds flavour and texture to the soup. Good to the last slurp.

✻ You may also like Bak Chor Mee, Fish Ball Noodles and Foochow Fish Ball Noodles.

6

BARBECUE CHICKEN WINGS

BBQ Chicken Wings are one of those things that your trusty nose would compel you towards. The aroma simply overrides fleshly resistance.

The birdie wings are marinated with shallots, garlic, ginger, dark soy sauce, white pepper, sesame oil, sugar and salt. Then they are grilled over open flame or charcoal, constantly rotated for an even 'tan'.

While the golden caramel skin is slightly charred to perfection, the meat remains juicy and tender. There is almost unbridled pleasure in biting through the crackling skin and into the firm meat. And as if that's not euphoric enough, dip the wing into the specially prepared chilli sauce after each bite to add a spicy and sour tang to the savoury meat. Savvy diners usually stand by a tall glass of iced lime juice as a cleansing foil to the oily treat.

* You may also like Char Siew, Roast Chicken and Roast Duck.

7

BEE HOON
BEE WHO-N

This is angel hair with a slender twist: it's much finer, and is made of rice. A common breakfast dish, Bee Hoon, also called Economy Bee Hoon, perhaps because its price is truly quite affordable, is simply rice vermicelli fried with salt or soya sauce. The noodles are kept quite plain, but are served with an assortment of tasty accompaniments, which you can choose, including fried luncheon meat slices, braised cabbage, deep-fried fish fillet, Otah (grilled fish paste), deep-fried egg and crispy chicken wings.

A popular version of this dish is Vegetarian Bee Hoon, where all accompaniments do not contain meat or meat products.

8

BEEF KWAY TEOW
BEEF KU-AY TI-OW

This dish is so tasty, you'll wish you were hungry just to enjoy it. Who can resist the flat, ribbon-like rice noodles served with tender sliced beef and minced beef balls? The dish also comes with internal parts such as tripe (cow's stomach) and tendons, salted vegetables, and bean sprouts. Usually, there's a choice of yellow noodles, called mee, or chor bee hoon (thick rice vermicelli). Some stalls serve the dish with a sprinkling of crushed peanuts and a half slice of fresh lime. Squeeze the lime into your garlic-laced chilli or noodles for a tangy punch. The soup packs oomph, being full of beef stock. Beef Kway Teow is also available "dry", meaning it is served with a thick, piquant gravy instead of soup. The "dry" version is also called Beef Noodles, or Dry Beef Noodles.

* *You may also like Char Kway Teow, Hokkien Mee, Hor Fun, Lor Mee and Mee Goreng.*

9

BEEF RENDANG
BEEF REHN-DAHNG

Initiate yourself into Malay culinary culture by indulging in this powerfully flavoured delicacy. The dish features beef chunks stewed in coconut milk and a spice paste of galangal, ginger, turmeric and lemon grass. The best Beef Rendang comprises melt-in-your-mouth beef that is clothed in a flavourful thick gravy of spices and coconut milk.

You will almost never find a hawker that sells only Beef Rendang. Instead, Beef Rendang is served at Nasi Padang stalls, which serve all kinds of delicious Malay cuisine. Beef Rendang is the showpiece entree for Nasi Padang.

* *You may also like Chicken Curry, Sayur Lodeh and Tauhu Telur.*

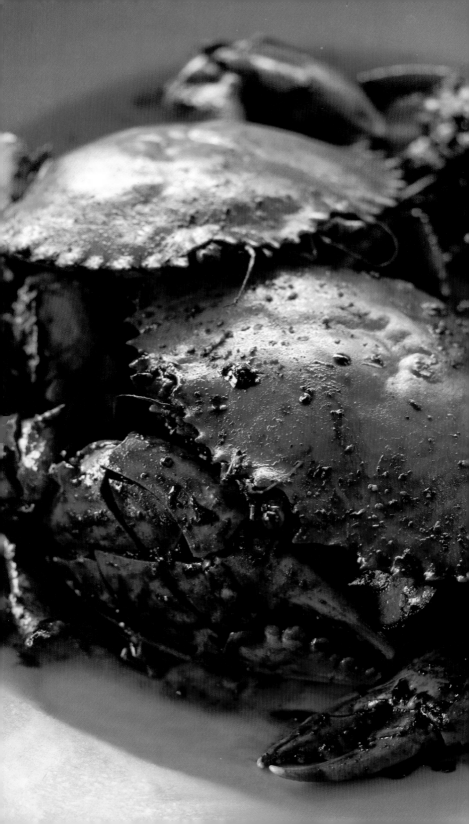

10

BLACK PEPPER CRAB

Black pepper brings out the character in crabs. Little wonder, this is one of the two most popular ways of serving crab in Singapore, the other being Chilli Crab. Black Pepper Crab uses hard-shell crabs that are first deep-fried, then mixed with a scrumptious black pepper sauce that comprises butter, garlic, oyster sauce, soya sauce and sugar. Sometimes, curry leaves or chilli are added to the sauce as well. To ensure the pepper is fiery hot, hawkers will roast or dry-fry the pepper before making the sauce. Locals love this dish for its pepper-crusted shells which provide a sharp contrast to the sweet and succulent meat inside. Best served with rice, baguette or deep-fried mantou (Chinese flour buns), eating crab is a messy affair, so ditch your forks, spoons, chopsticks and table manners, and dig in with your fingers!

* You may also like Chilli Crab.

SINGAPORE CLASSIC

11

CARROT CAKE

This is not the sweet carrot-laden dessert of Western origin. In fact, there are no carrots in local Carrot Cake. Instead this savoury dish is made by steaming grated white radish (also known as white carrot in Chinese) and rice flour till a coagulated shape is achieved. The cake is then broken into chunks and stir-fried till slightly charred. Egg, soya sauce, white pepper and chilli sauce are added, with spring onions serving as garnish.

You can order Carrot Cake "white" or "black". The blackened version is generously doused with a thick dark sweet soya sauce, while the white version contains only a sprinkling of the sauce. Carrot Cake is a popular dish for sharing with friends. It can be eaten for breakfast, as a snack or as part of a dim sum spread.

* You may also like Char Siew Bao, Chee Cheong Fun, Egg Tart and Lo Mai Kai.

SINGAPORE ★ CLASSIC

12

CHAPATI
CHAH-PAH-THI

It looks like a pan-seared UFO – sans the yeast – and tastes anything but flat. Chapati is an Indian unleavened wholemeal bread. Thinner than a pita, Chapati is served with meat or vegetable curries. It is made of very fine wholemeal flour, ghee (clarified butter) and warm water. When served, it is a pale beige, often with burnt black spots all over.

Chapati can be eaten the local way – with your hands – or with a knife and fork. Why not have some fun and improvise by using Chapati to wrap your favourite choice of meat: roast chicken or beef, rosemary lamb, or tandoori chicken.

* ***You may also like Murtabak, Roti Prata and Roti John.***

13

CHAR KWAY TEOW
CHAR KU-AY TI-OW

To describe this dish as mere stir-fried Chinese flat noodles seems somewhat of an insult. This classic Singapore dish is essentially that, but so much more. For one, the frying takes place in a scorching, sizzling cast iron wok. The delectable smell of hot oil, garlic and crispy fried pork fat, diced and flung in, is everywhere while kway teow (white flat rice noodles) with some mee (thick yellow noodles) are thrown in, together with slices of lapcheong (waxed Chinese sausage), bean sprouts and fish cake (slices of fish paste). Some seafood, like shrimp, sotong (squid) or even cockles, are also added. There is also the signature cracking of an egg (or two) into the mixture, followed by vigorous stirring and mixing in of the sauce – usually a combination of dark and light soya sauces and oyster sauce – until all is cooked and ready to be served, piping hot.

Char Kway Teow is typically served on a plate, with a dollop of chilli paste and a small cut lime on the side (for you to squeeze over the darkened noodle dish before digging in).

* *You may also like Beef Kway Teow, Hokkien Mee, Hor Fun, Lor Mee and Mee Goreng.*

SINGAPORE CLASSIC

CHAR SIEW BAO
CHAR SEE-YOO BOW

The Western equivalent of this unique treat is... non-existent. This Chinese dim sum delight comprises a steamed flour bun stuffed with roast pork filling that is often dyed bright red with food colouring. The dough of the bun ranges from being light, fluffy, and almost cake-like, to being thin and bread-like, depending on the hawker. The char siew (roast pork) filling is often juicy and sweet.

Char Siew Bao is a favourite snack among locals. Although rare, some hawkers still make their own Char Siew Bao from scratch. Such handmade buns are a cut above the typical factory-made buns you will find most hawkers selling. Still, be it handmade or factory-made, Char Siew Bao is a firm favourite with virtually every visitor to Singapore.

You may also like Ang Ku Kueh, Carrot Cake, Chee Cheong Fun, Chwee Kueh, Egg Tart, Lo Mai Kai, Muah Chee and Soon Kueh.

CHAR SIEW RICE
CHAR SEE-YOO RICE

Few dishes induce hunger like this one. Slices of tender pork, marinated and roasted to perfection, are served atop white rice and doused with a thick sweet gravy. The pork is usually a little fatty – roasted fat makes the pork slightly sweet – and some charred bits are common too, as locals like the crisp texture of slightly burnt pork. Char Siew Rice is often served with a few slices of cucumber.

You will seldom find a hawker selling Char Siew Rice exclusively. Instead, Char Siew Rice is often sold at the "Roast Meats" or "Roast Duck Meat" stall. It is very common to order a variety of roast meats and share it among friends, e.g., instead of just ordering Char Siew Rice, try ordering Char Siew and Roast Duck, and ask for the rice to be served separately. This combination of roast meats, eaten with rice, is simply divine! Wanton Soup or Prawn Dumpling Soup is often ordered as a fitting side dish to complement the meal.

* *You may also like Roast Duck Rice.*

CHEE CHEONG FUN
CHEE CHONG FAHN

This is another Chinese treat with no counterpart in the West. Chee Cheong Fun is made of thin rice sheets that are rolled up and served with a thick sweet sauce. Rice flour and water are poured into flat pans and steamed to produce the thin rice sheet. The translucent white sheet is then rolled up plain, or with "stuffing", usually shrimp or Char Siew (roast pork), and then sliced into bite-sized pieces. A thick sweet sauce, sesame oil and sesame seeds are used to season the rice roll. Alternatively, Chee Cheong Fun can be served with soya sauce, spring onions and chilli sauce.

Chee Cheong Fun is known for its light, soft, melt-in-your-mouth texture and is often taken for breakfast, as a snack or as part of a dim sum spread.

* *You may also like Ang Ku Kueh, Carrot Cake, Char Siew Bao, Chwee Kueh, Egg Tart, Lo Mai Kai, Muah Chee and Soon Kueh.*

CHICKEN CURRY

For those who are not too chicken to try exotic spices, this stew packs a wallop. This heartwarming home favourite is great to eat any day, any time. Chicken pieces are stir-fried in a seasoning paste that contains turmeric, nutmeg, cinnamon, coriander and cumin. Coconut milk is added for flavour and oomph and sometimes, potato chunks are used to thicken the curry. The result – tender, soft chicken swathed in a rich, heartwarming gravy. Heaven.

Chicken Curry is best eaten with steamed rice or baguette to soak up the sort of gravy you won't forget in a hurry.

Like Beef Rendang, you will almost never find a hawker that sells Chicken Curry alone. Instead, Chicken Curry is served at Nasi Padang and Economy Rice stalls.

* You may also like Beef Rendang, Sayur Lodeh and Tauhu Telur.

18

CHICKEN RICE

It looks plain but tastes profound. The chicken is cooked in boiling water and then steeped briefly in ice water. It is served together with steamed rice that has been cooked in chicken stock and chicken fat. Dark soya sauce, special chilli sauce and ginger sauce complement the dish. Chicken Rice is also known as Hainanese Chicken Rice as this Chinese dialect group is said to have created this lovely dish.

Kampong Chicken Rice is a variety of Chicken Rice made from free-range chicken that is leaner and tastier.

The best Chicken Rice has flavourful rice that is so tasty, it can be eaten on its own. The chicken meat should be tender and succulent, without being overly oily, and the chilli and ginger sauces must provide sufficient kick to bring out the flavour of the chicken, without overpowering it. When ordering Chicken Rice, you may be asked if you want white/steamed or dark/roasted meat. "Dark" means the chicken skin has been roasted. Order the classic "white" meat Chicken Rice, and pair it with Lime Juice and Prawn Dumpling Soup, for a classic street food meal!

19

CHILLI CRAB

Revered for more than its fiery looks, the Chilli Crab is considered a national dish by many. The key to Chilli Crab is the hearty, thick, sweet and spicy gravy, a combination of tomato sauce, chilli sauce, lime juice and egg. To give more spicy oomph, bright red chilli padi is thrown into the mix – chilli padi is the hottest form of chilli there is here. The result – a bright red hard-shell crab encrusting sweet and succulent meat, but covered with a mouth-watering gravy that is usually very quickly mopped up with rice, baguette or deep-fried mantou (Chinese flour buns). Chilli Crab is one of the two most popular ways of serving crab in Singapore, the other being Black Pepper Crab. But why choose when you can shell-shock your system with both?

✻ You may also like Black Pepper Crab.

20

CHINESE ROJAK
CHINESE ROW-JAHK

It's black and messy, but what a marvellous mess! A veritable mix of sweet, sour, salty, crunchy, juicy and spicy, Chinese Rojak – "rojak" meaning "mixture" in Malay – is in essence, a fruit and vegetable salad, Southeast Asian style! Bite-sized chunks of cucumber and pineapple are mixed with red or green chillies and tossed with a unique dressing – a fiesty brew of hae ko (dried shrimp paste), vinegar or tamarind, sugar, salt and lemon juice – and topped with chopped peanuts. Truly a unique combination. Sometimes, ingredients like you tiao (deep-fried dough crullers) and tau pok (puffy tofu cubes) are also added.

Chinese Rojak and Indian Rojak are like day and night, with little similarity except for the fact that both are "mixtures" of a variety of ingredients.

* *You may also like Indian Rojak.*

21

CHWEE KUEH
CH-WEE KU-AY

Being a staple in the Asian diet, rice is prepared in countless ingenious ways. Here's one that features radish as you have never tasted it before. Rice flour and water are mixed and steamed in small cups, similar in size and shape to the muffin moulds used for baking. The result is a springy, moist, soft "cake" that is tasteless on its own, but topped with mouth-watering condiments – chai poh (diced preserved radish bits), which is crunchy, salty-sweet and oily. Minced garlic, fried shallots and toasted sesame seeds are also added. Chwee Kueh is often taken with chilli sauce and is a favourite breakfast food and snack.

* You may also like Ang Ku Kueh, Char Siew Bao, Chee Cheong Fun, Muah Chee and Soon Kueh.

22

CLAYPOT RICE

The Spanish have paella; the Chinese, Claypot Rice. As the name suggests, rice is cooked in a claypot and when almost done, chunks of juicy chicken, slices of Chinese mushrooms and slivers of lapcheong (waxed Chinese sausage) are spread on top and cooked together with steamed rice. Dark soya sauce, oyster sauce, sesame oil and spring onions add flavour to this dish, which is considered a real comfort food. The best Claypot Rice has rice grains that are not entirely stained with dark soya sauce. And if you think the black and white grains of rice are delicious, you haven't tasted the burnt ones encrusted on the inside of the claypot!

23

CRAB TANG HOON
CRAB TAHNG WHO-N

Sit down with a Singapore family over a seafood spread, and you're likely to find this dish being one of the centrestage dishes. A very unique dish, a whole crab is stir-fried in garlic and butter, then braised in a milky soup. Tang hoon (glass noodles) is added and the result – a robust seafood noodle dish with a sweet buttery taste. Not forgetting a whole, bright red crab beckoning you to dig in.

This dish is sometimes prepared in a claypot and for extra oomph, X.O., meaning extra-old brandy, is added. (Hawkers may use regular brandy, instead of extra-old brandy.) The dish can also be prepared with bee hoon, in which case, it would be called Crab Bee Hoon.

❋ You may also like Fish Bee Hoon and Sliced Fish Noodle Soup.

24

CURRY FISH HEAD

The best way to a man's heart is through the head – the fish head. A distinctly Singaporean dish, an entire fish head – usually that of a snapper, garoupa or bream – is cooked in a spicy, sour, watery curry that comprises spices like tamarind, coriander, cumin, fennel, turmeric and fenugeek. Coconut milk is added for fragrance. Apart from the fish head, vegetables like okra, eggplant and tomatoes are also added. But don't let all this distract you from the real thrill of eating Curry Fish Head – finding the elusive fish brain, and yes, digging out and sucking on the gelatinous eyeballs. This is Fear Factor eating at its best, but most of all, this dish is truly scrumptious, especially with steamed white rice!

Tiger Beer is the perfect complement to this dish.

SINGAPORE CLASSIC

25

CURRY PUFF

Here is a pie that is knotty and nice. Similar to the Western meat pie, this all-time favourite snack is a savoury meat dumpling, shaped like a semi-circle and with knotted edges. The outer dough is deep-fried till crisp and serves as a skin for curried filling, usually spicy chicken, potato cubes and slices of hard-boiled eggs.

Recently, inventive hawkers have begun putting more interesting fillings in Curry Puffs, including spicy sardines and non-spicy options, like sweet corn, and even the most enigmatic of fruits – durian. Look out for it!

The Malay version of Curry Puff is called Epok Epok.

You may also like Goreng Pisang and You Tiao.

DUCK RICE

This dish is not to be confused with Roast Duck Rice, an altogether different animal that deserves a whole other entry. Duck Rice, also known as Boneless Duck Rice, Braised Duck Rice, Teochew Duck Rice or Stewed Duck Rice features a whole duck, marinated with five-spice powder, dark and light soya sauces and galangal. The duck is then placed in a large wok and browned with caramelised sugar before it is braised together with garlic and cinnamon.

The result? Thin, tender, brown slices of duck served atop steamed white rice and moistened with the braising sauce. Guaranteed no lame duck.

ECONOMY RICE

The Economy Rice stall, found in every hawker centre and food court in the country, often sets the hungry stomach rumbling just by the visual feast of Chinese dishes displayed. You will find all sorts of mostly non-spicy meat and vegetable options here – stir-fried leafy green local vegetables cooked with garlic, braised soya sauce chicken, steamed fish, steamed egg, braised soya sauce fatty pork slices, sweet and sour pork, lemon chicken and steamed tofu are but some local favourites. It is up to you to choose what you would like and the dishes are served with rice, or sometimes, fried rice or bee hoon (rice vermicelli). Take your pick.

It is common for pricing to be based on calculations like "2 meat + 1 vegetable", "1 meat + 2 vegetable" and so on. In addition, after ordering, the hawker will ask if you would like to add some gravy to your dish, be it brown meat gravy (either pork or chicken) or spicy curry gravy.

This dish is also called Chinese Mixed Rice, Curry Rice or Hainanese Curry Rice. The Malay version of this dish, with spicier accompaniments, is Nasi Padang.

* You may also like Roast Duck Rice.

EGG TART

Egg Tarts were originally intended only for the Chinese Emperor. Commoners today would be forgiven for thinking of flan or quiche the moment they set eyes on this "royal" pastry. Egg Tarts are lovely as snacks, desserts or dim sum items. They comprise a smooth silken egg custard so delicate that it wobbles ever so slightly when shaken. This creamy sweet mixture is encased in shortcrust pastry or flaky puff pastry, a buttery and crisp complement to the quivering custard. They are small enough to be eaten in two or three bites.

Portuguese Egg Tarts are distinct because the egg custard has signature dark brown burnt spots that crater over its surface, similar to the caramelised surface of crème brulee. Agreeable enough to send you over the moon, Egg Tarts go well with coffee.

✳ You may also like Ang Ku Kueh, Carrot Cake, Chee Cheong Fun, Char Siew Bao, Chwee Kueh, Lo Mai Kai, Muah Chee and Soon Kueh.

29

FISH BALL NOODLES

Add some bounce to your eating adventure; try this noodle dish, with fish balls as the prime ingredient. These are bite-sized balls fashioned from fish meat that has been vigorously pounded into a paste. After being cooked, they are soft and succulent. Besides fish balls, other ingredients include minced pork and braised sliced mushrooms.

You will be given a choice of noodles – bee hoon (rice vermicelli), mee kia (thin yellow noodles, similar to angel-hair spaghetti), mee pok (flat yellow noodles, similar to fettuccine) or mee (thick egg noodles). You will also be asked whether you would like the dish "soup" or "dry" and will be given a choice: whether to add chilli or not.

* You may also like Crab Tang Hoon and Sliced Fish Noodle Soup.

30

FISH BEE HOON
FISH BEE WHO-N

When it comes to favourite hawker foods, this dish scales the heights. Fish Bee Hoon is a noodle soup dish that has an intensely flavourful milky soup as its base. Thick or thin rice vermicelli, also know as bee hoon or chor bee hoon, are topped with fish slices that are freshly blanched or deep-fried. Sometimes, you can also ask for a fish head – eyes, gills, cheeks and all. For a tinge of sweetness and added body, X.O., meaning extra-old brandy, is added. (Hawkers may use regular brandy, instead of extra-old brandy.) So don't eat and drive.

* You may also like Bak Chor Mee, Ban Mian and
Foochow Fish Ball Noodles.

FOOCHOW
FISH BALL NOODLES

Fish balls are commonly cooked in southern China and overseas Chinese communities. As the name suggests, the ball is made of fish meat that has been finely pulverised. All bones have been removed, so there's little danger of choking (provided you bite instead of swallowing it whole)! And size does matter, at least for these Foochow (a port in southeastern China) balls. After all, these oddly pudgy delicacies, resembling ping pong balls, are stuffed with minced pork. They are soft and al dente, and the minced pork is still juicy and soft inside. You can choose the type of noodles you would like to eat this dish with, though most locals would order bee hoon (rice vermicelli) or mee kia (thin yellow noodles, similar to angel-hair spaghetti).

Ask for less oil and more vegetables. But never less fish balls as they are so good you can eat them on their own. Dip each one in a little soya sauce for a big taste.

✴ You may also like Bak Chor Mee, Ban Mian and Fish Ball Noodles.

32

GORENG PISANG
GO-RING PEE-SAHNG

Most locals go bananas over this snack. Goreng Pisang is Malay for "frying a banana". Also known as Pisang Goreng, this is a lovely snack food of fried banana fritters – whole bananas are dipped in a smooth batter of flour and water and then deep-fried to golden perfection. Potassium never tasted so good. And if you like this, you might also like other fruity options including sweet potato, mashed green bean, jackfruit and tapioca.

If you're a weight watcher, all is not lost. You can still go for Goreng Pisang by removing the fried batter, eating only the naturally sugared, nutritious fruit. Enjoy a delicious twist by adding low-fat ice cream or frozen yoghurt. In any case, don't leave Singapore without eating a dozen of these golden delights.

* You may also like Curry Puff and You Tiao.

33

HOKKIEN MEE
HOCK-KEE-N MEE

Yet another perennial favourite, this noodle dish comprises mee (thick yellow noodles) and bee hoon (rice vermicelli) stir-fried with shrimp, bean sprouts, fish cake (slices of fish paste), sotong (squid) and sometimes, chicken or pork. The best renditions of Hokkien Mee are neither completely dry nor completely soupy, but somewhere in between. The noodles are stir-fried with pork lard. Towards the end, an egg is cracked in and mixed around before shrimp (or sometimes, pork or seafood) stock is scooped in. The noodles are allowed to braise for a while, soaking up the goodness of the stock, before they are served. The result – a tantalisingly gooey (but not mushy), slurpy delicious noodle dish with minimal gravy, yet still moist and mouth-watering.

Hokkien Mee is served with a scoop of chilli paste and a small cut lime on the side. Sometimes, the dish is served on a beige/light brown soft palm bark which has a slight fragrance.

* You may also like Beef Kway Teow, Char Kway Teow, Hor Fun, Lor Mee and Mee Goreng.

HONG CHAO JI
HONG JOW JEE

Is this the local version of coq au vin, the famous French chicken stew with red wine? Almost, but not quite. This humble red wine chicken stew comprises chicken marinated in red rice wine and ginger, and braised till tender and succulent. The stew has a distinctive bright red colour, courtesy of the red rice wine. Its robust flavour and fragrance, due to the wine, makes it a heartwarming dish. Hong Chao Ji is usually served with rice or mee sua (very fine rice noodles).

Chances are you'll not only finish eating the chicken meat, but also drink up every drop of that delicious wine-soup. You can ask for more soup, but manage your expectations as it takes a while to cook the health-enhancing soup for Hong Chao Ji.

35

HOR FUN
HOR FAHN

Much broader than tagliatelle in width and flavour, this noodle dish uses kway teow (white flat rice noodles) that are stir-fried and darkened with soya sauce. Shrimp, sotong (squid), pork slices, green leafy vegetables and fish cake (slices of fish paste) are added.

The noodles are then immersed in a dark, thick bean sauce gravy. Hawkers will sometimes give you a choice of chicken, pork or seafood when you order Hor Fun.

There are also two special forms of Hor Fun that have earned a loyal following of their own – Beef Hor Fun is a favourite among locals for the delectable combination of super-tender, thin, fried beef slices placed over noodles and doused in a scrumptious black bean sauce. San Lao Hor Fun is also another favourite – unlike other forms of Hor Fun, the kway teow is kept "white", not darkened with soya sauce, and is served with fresh fish slices, lots of spring onions and bean sprouts.

* You may also like Beef Kway Teow, Char Kway Teow, Hokkien Mee, Ipoh Hor Fun, Lor Mee or Mee Goreng.

36

INDIAN ROJAK
INDIAN ROW-JAHK

Not to be confused with Chinese Rojak is Indian Rojak. Common ingredients for this salad include potato chunks, fried tofu, coconut flour balls, prawn fritters, vegetable fritters, fried sotong (squid) and cuttlefish, sambal eggs (boiled eggs covered with spicy chilli paste) and fried tempe (fermented soya bean cake). Everything in Indian Rojak is fried or deep-fried. "Rojak" means mixture in Malay.

Indian Rojak is different from Chinese Rojak in that you are expected to pick what you want to include when you order. The hawker will then freshly re-fry all chosen ingredients and serve everything crispy and piping hot, with a signature orange-coloured sweet chilli dip that is made of mashed sweet potatoes, tamarind, chilli powder, sugar, salt and toasted sesame seeds.

＊*You may also like Satay Bee Hoon.*

37

IPOH HOR FUN
EE-POE HOR FAHN

Everything looks white and bland, but don't believe your eyes. Not only does this dish go down well with the locals, it goes down smoothly. Ipoh (a city in Malaysia) Hor Fun is known for its super soft, silky kway teow (white flat rice noodles) that are usually less wide than the kway teow used in Hor Fun. These thin, slippery noodles are so soft, they almost melt in your mouth. Ipoh Hor Fun is usually served with tender chicken strips, braised mushrooms and green leafy vegetables. It is considered a light dish since the noodles are not very filling. Of course, the delicious news is that you can order Ipoh Hor Fun and still sample other dishes that catch your fancy!

Some hawker centres, food courts and restaurants offer Ipoh Hor Fun with crayfish. The whole crayfish – all of seven inches, tender and tasting somewhat like lobster – is cut vertically in half so you can easily remove the meat without breaking sweat.

* *You may also like Hor Fun.*

38

KAYA TOAST
KAH-YAH TOAST

Spread the news around: Kaya is a uniquely Southeast Asian jam made from coconut milk and eggs, flavoured by pandan leaf and sweetened with sugar. This coconut egg jam has a lovely sweet and creamy flavour and can be either brown or green, depending on the proportion of pandan (which is green) and the extent of the caramelisation of sugar.

Kaya is spread on toast and served as a breakfast food. Also known as Kaya Roti or Roti Kaya, it can also be enjoyed as a snack throughout the day. Kaya Toast is usually accompanied by two soft boiled eggs, and Kopi (local black coffee) or Teh (tea).

39

KUEH PIE TEE
KU-AY PIE TEE

You have to take your hat off to these little buggers. Affectionately known as top hats, these delightful hors d'oeuvres rank high in flavour and presentation. A crispy case of deep-fried batter is filled with slightly crunchy yet juicy shredded turnip and topped with bits of crab meat, shrimp, lettuce, roasted peanuts and egg. Coriander leaves and spring onions are used as garnish and the dish is served with a sweet chilli sauce.

Kueh Pie Tee is often eaten as a snack or shared with friends as a side dish.

* You may also like Popiah.

40

KUEH TU TU
KU-AY TOO TOO

Supple. Round. Flat. The texture is wonderfully chewy, without being rubbery. Bite-sized delicacies that could be either sweet or savoury, these steamed rice flour cakes have a soft, snowy-white skin that is made from rice flour. You can choose between a filling of either coarsely chopped toasted peanuts or grated coconut that has been dry-fried till fragrant and moistened with gula melaka (palm sugar).

Kueh Tu Tu is a traditional Singapore delicacy that is often eaten as a feel-good snack.

41

KWAY CHAP
KU-AY CH-AHP

Steel yourself, order this dish and pig out. These wide, white flat rice noodles, also called kway teow, are cooked in a palatable herbal soya-based broth, and is accompanied by a plate of pig's organs. Yes, make no mistake: pig's organs are the main feature of this dish, including the inner lining of a pig's stomach, intestines, and even, the ears, skin and tongue! Other "forms" of pork include belly pork and lean pork. Other ingredients include tofu cubes and boiled eggs.

Although this sounds bizarre and thoroughly unappetising, it is amazing to taste how delicious a soup of pig parts can be. Kway Chap, often eaten for breakfast, is known as a heartwarming dish and is often served with chilli sauce for added bite.

42

LAKSA
LUCK-SAH

This rich-in-flavour spicy noodle soup dish has abundant ground-up dried shrimp in its gravy, giving it an almost sandy texture. The key to Laksa is the gravy. It is made by pounding chillies, shallots, galangal, garlic, ginger, lemon grass, turmeric, candlenuts and hae ko (dried shrimp paste). The resulting spice mix is fried in oil before coconut milk and shrimp stock are added. Mee tai mak (round thick white noodles) or chor bee hoon (thick rice vermicelli) are added together with tau pok (puffy tofu cubes), shrimp, bean sprouts and raw cockles. Poshed up versions even come with quail's eggs, tiger prawns and scallops!

Unlike Singapore-style Laksa, which is also known as Laksa Lemak, Penang-style Laksa has a watery spicy-sour fish gravy made of fish stock. The rempah is served in a separate bowl for you to add, unlike Singapore-style Laksa.

According to "Singapore: The Encyclopedia", the name Laksa is derived from a Sanskrit word meaning "many".

❋ You may also like Lontong and Mee Siam.

LO MAI KAI
LOR MY GAI

The name may leave your tongue in knots but the taste promises pleasure. "Lo mai" means glutinous rice, while "kai" means chicken. This savoury dish wrapped in lotus leaf is a dim sum favourite comprising steamed glutinous rice with juicy chicken pieces, Chinese mushrooms and lapcheong (waxed Chinese sausage). A takeaway version can also be found at hawker centres and food courts – instead of a lotus leaf, a small round aluminium tray is used to hold the dish together.

The glutinous rice of Lo Mai Kai is flavourful because it has absorbed the juices and flavours of the chicken, mushroom and lapcheong. Lo Mai Kai is served steaming hot as a side dish, snack or as an early morning dim sum treat. It goes well with a cleansing cup of hot Chinese tea or hot Japanese green tea, as Lo Mai Kai tends to be oily. Rice and shine!

* You may also like Ang Ku Kueh, Carrot Cake, Char Siew Bao, Chee Cheong Fun, Chwee Kueh, Egg Tart and Soon Kueh.

44

LONTONG
LONG-TONG

Here's a spicy soupy Malay favourite that's short on presentation but long on taste. Made from mashed rice and shaped into flat rectangular pieces, Lontong comes with a signature yellow gravy that is coconut milk-based. Vegetables like French beans and cabbage, as well as tofu and boiled eggs, are braised in the gravy, together with the steamed rice cakes. Toasted grated coconut is added on top for additional fragrance and flavour.

The texture is creamy and smooth, the colour really appetising, and the taste hard to fault. Lontong may look lightweight but with a balanced diet of carbohydrates and proteins, it's a full meal in itself. All this, for about $3.00 or less. What a steal!

* *You may also like Laksa and Mee Siam.*

45

LOR MEE
LAW MEE

It's sticky, it's yummy and it's all-in-one. No wonder some foodies drive for miles just to patronise their favourite stall serving this dish. The thick yellow noodles, called mee, are coated with a unique (among hawker fare in Singapore, at least) thick brown gravy that makes the noodles glide down your throat. Toppings include fish cake (slices of fish paste), wantons (dumplings), boiled eggs, shrimp, char siew (roast pork), ngoh hiang (deep-fried pork spring rolls), pork belly and even, deep-fried fish fritters. Toss and mix well before you hungrily dig in. Add some black vinegar and chilli to inject zing into the overall experience.

And because the gravy is thick with flavour, you'll do well to have a glass of ice-cold beer within grabbing distance. You may quench your thirst but not necessarily the desire to return for more.

* You may also like Beef Kway Teow, Char Kway Teow, Hokkien Mee, Hor Fun, Lor Mee and Mee Goreng.

46

MEE GORENG
MEE GO-RING

Indian-inspired, multi-racially appreciated. This delicious dish of spicy fried noodles is cooked up by Indian-Muslim hawkers and is a fine example of the liberal intermingling of ideas and influences in the Singapore kitchen.

Chinese yellow fresh egg noodles, called mee, are stir-fried with (Indian) curry leaves, chillies and cubes of potato, tofu and tomatoes. A mix of dark sweet soya sauce, chilli paste and ketchup is added to give the noodle dish its signature sour, spicy, sweet and tangy flavour. A great fusion dish that is perfect for vegetarians. Sometimes, this dish is fried up with kway teow noodles, which are wide and flat. The dish is called Kway Teow Goreng.

✱ You may also like Beef Kway Teow, Char Kway Teow, Hokkien Mee, Hor Fun and Lor Mee.

47

MEE REBUS
MEE REH-BOOS

For this Malay specialty, the oomph lies in the stiff, temperature-hot gravy: creamy, nutty, habit-forming. The gravy is made from aromatic spices like galangal, candlenuts, chilli, coriander powder and taucheo (salted soya beans). Chinese yellow fresh egg noodles, called mee, are drenched in this gratifying gravy thickened with sweet potato. Mix well or the noodles could taste bland.

On the other hand, once mixed thoroughly, Mee Rebus tastes faintly sweet (but far from cloying) and spicy, with a delicate tang of the exotic Malay Peninsula. It may not be food for Malay royalty, but the dish is manifestly ethnic and enticing. Squeeze the half lime into the noodles for extra zest. Sambal chilli is a delicious option.

✱ You may also like Soto Ayam.

48

MEE SIAM
MEE SEE-AHM

This simple noodle dish of stir-fried bee hoon – if you consider a heady blend of sweet, spicy and sour notes simple – is dressed up with spicy, sweet and sour flavours that make it a crowd-pleasing hawker favourite. The secret is in the spice paste – a pounded mix of chillies, shallots, candlenuts, taucheo (salted soya beans) and sugar. Shrimp stock forms the base and the sour kick comes from the tamarind.

Mee Siam is served two ways – dry or with gravy. Both versions are distinctively orange in colour and are topped with cubes of deep-fried tofu, slices of hard-boiled eggs and fish cake (slices of fish paste), with chilli paste and a slice of cut lime served on the side.

The origin of Mee Siam may be Malay, but its appeal is universal – at least in Singapore it is.

* *You may also like Laksa and Lontong.*

49

MUAH CHEE
MOO-AH CHEE

Things are going to get sticky but not tacky. And you're going to love it. A marshmallow-look-alike (but please don't roast it over an open fire!), Muah Chee is a chewy confection quite similar to the well-loved Japanese mochi. Glutinous rice flour, sugar, water and oil are mixed together and steamed to form a faintly sweet chewy dough that is then cut up into smaller pieces and liberally tossed in toasted ground peanuts and topped with sesame seeds.

The unique combination of chewy and crunchy – the chewiness of the glutinous rice and the crunchiness of the toasted peanuts – makes Muah Chee a sought-after local snack; it's hard not to develop a soft spot for these nibbles.

They are fondly eaten with toothpicks, but try picking them up with your fingers to feel the cotton-soft texture.

You may also like Ang Ku Kueh, Char Siew Bao, Chee Cheong Fun, Chwee Kueh and Soon Kueh.

50

MURTABAK
MUR-TAH-BAHK

Sandwich doesn't even begin to describe this flavour-packed Indian-Muslim food. Murtabak is an unleavened bread, like pita, that is fried till crisp and golden, and filled with minced chicken, mutton, vegetables or egg. It is served with steaming curry and eaten with a fork and spoon.

Achieving the roti (bread) is a magical sight to watch. The hawker will take little lumps of dough and with the muscular grace of a danseur, a male ballerina, he will begin to fling the handful of dough in ever-widening circular motion, until a rather large thin sheet of dough is achieved. The dough is slapped onto a hot griddle, whereupon fillings are added. You may request the fillings you want: chicken, mutton or sardine. Extra onions? No problem.

Something very similar to Murtabak is Roti Prata – a smaller version of the Murtabak that can be eaten plain or with filling. But never with indifference.

* *You may also like Chapati, Roti Prata and Roti John.*

51

NASI BIRYANI
NAH-SEE BRR-YAH-NEE

How can anyone resist long-grain, delicately fragrant basmati rice, gently fried with ghee (clarified butter) and spices like cinnamon, cloves, cardamom, onions, ginger and garlic? That's not all. It is then boiled in a meaty stock, usually with either chicken or mutton bones, with raisins, cashews, coriander and shallots added. Yellow or orange food colouring is sometimes added to give the rice a festive-looking tinge.

Nasi Biryani is sometimes also called Biryani or Dum Biryani (in this version, the chicken is cooked with the rice, not separately). "Nasi" is actually the Malay word for "rice". This Indian-Muslim dish is often served with a meat curry, e.g., lamb curry (lamb biryani) or chicken curry (chicken biryani).

✱ *You may also like Nasi Padang.*

52

NASI GORENG
NAH-SEE GO-RING

Nasi Goreng is Malay for "fried rice", "nasi" meaning rice in Malay. A local take on the paella, it is prepared with pre-cooked rice. The rice is cooked ahead of time and allowed to cool so that the rice is not soggy. The rice is stir-fried with egg and shrimp, and spiced with chilli (especially for the Indonesian version, called Nasi Goreng Istimewa), tamarind, soya sauce, garlic, fried shallots and spring onions.

Additional items perk up this exotic dish, like a nice egg sunny side up, lip-smacking fried chicken (trust the Malays to do great fried chicken), a few sticks of succulent satay (skewered chicken, beef or lamb; never pork), several slices of cool cucumber and tomatoes, and two large pieces of crackling prawn crackers. Who says a balanced meal is a boring meal?

❊ *You may also like Nasi Lemak and Nasi Padang.*

53

NASI LEMAK
NAH-SEE LEH-MAHK

Are you ready for rice cream? Yes, rice cream. Nasi Lemak means "rice in cream" in Malay. This popular dish comprises rice that is cooked in coconut milk, making it irresistibly fragrant. The rice is served with deep-fried crispy ikan bilis (dried anchovies), roasted peanuts, sliced cucumbers, a fried egg or boiled egg, and a crispy deep-fried chicken wing or drumstick. Sambal accompanies this lovely dish that is popular for breakfast as well as any time of the day!

Foodies will often judge a hawker's Nasi Lemak by the quality of his sambal, the fragrance of the coconut rice and the crispiness of the fried chicken. Nasi Lemak is eaten with a fork and spoon, or with your hands. Use only the right hand to observe table etiquette.

✻ You may also like Nasi Goreng and Nasi Padang.

54

NASI PADANG
NAH-SEE PAH-DAHNG

Nasi Padang means "rice from Padang", Padang being a place in West Sumatra. But in hawker-speak, Nasi Padang more generically refers to Malay-Muslim food. A Nasi Padang stall will typically serve a stunning array of fragrant spicy curries (wet, soupy), rendangs (dry, more gravy than soup) and sambals (items covered in chilli paste and fried) which you can choose to eat with white rice. Here are some must-order items: Beef Rendang, Chicken Curry, crispy fried chicken, sambal shrimp (chilli-fried shrimp), Sayur Lodeh (vegetables braised in coconut milk), Tauhu Telur and stir-fried spicy calamari.

It is common for Nasi Padang to be shared communally. Instead of piling the meat and vegetables atop individual plates of rice, you can ask the hawker to serve you portions enough for a few people, in separate plates.

*** You may also like Economy Rice, Nasi Goreng and Nasi Lemak.**

55

NGOH HIANG
NOR HEE-ONG

Cut the crab and stuff it – in a spring roll. But more than crabmeat, this is a spring roll, using beancurd as the skin, with minced chicken or pork seasoned with five-spice powder as delicious filling. The roll is steamed first, then deep-fried till crispy. The insides remain moist. This Hokkien/Teochew specialty is served with chilli sauce and black sauce. Goes well with a bowl of steamed white rice. A typical Ngoh Hiang stall will often serve more than just this yummy five-spice roll. You will be able to choose from an array of deep-fried snacks, including prawn fritters, fish cake (slices of fish paste) and even stuffed Chinese sausages.

Ngoh Hiang is sometimes taken as a snack. It can also be found in Economy Rice stalls or stalls selling Teochew Porridge. Many stalls in Singaporean food courts and hawker centres sell fried bee hoon with Ngoh Hiang; this combination is a favourite for many from breakfast through supper!

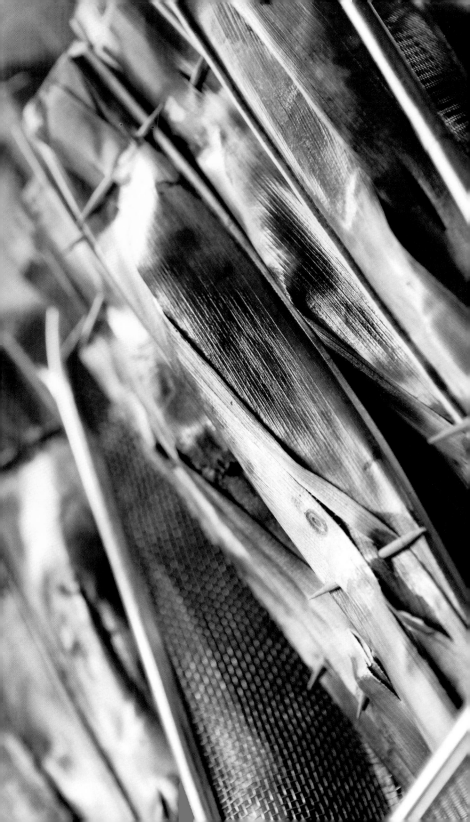

56

OTAH
OH-TAH

Seafood over charcoal fire never fails, especially when it's Otah. Otah comprises fish meat that is ground into a paste and seasoned with a rempah of chilli, turmeric, candlenuts, lemon grass and coriander. Coconut milk is added to keep the fish paste moist before it is wrapped in banana leaf and grilled over a charcoal fire. When unwrapped, the fish meat has a tell-tale reddish-orange colour and a delectable smoky seafood aroma. Tastewise, it has the consistency of a savoury mousse.

In Singapore, creative hawkers have taken Otah to another level by coming up with innovative Otah ingredients, including fish head, sotong (squid), shrimp, fish roe, crab and even, non-spicy seafood versions. Not all hawkers have these innovations, so be on the look out and try them out if you come across them. Whatever the ingredient, Otah is great with white bread, rice, or on its own.

✳ You may also like Sambal Stingray.

57

OYSTER OMELETTE

If you like oysters and eggs, scramble to the nearest hawker centre for this curious-looking delicacy. This dish, though called an omelette, rarely retains the shape of an omelette as there are more oysters and filling ingredients – like bean sprouts – than egg batter. Starch is also added to the egg batter to make it thicker. The result – a delectable marriage of just-cooked oysters and somewhat crisp and slightly browned egg, seasoned with salt, pepper and coriander.

Also known as Or Luak or Or Chiaan, Oyster Omelette is a great dish for sharing with friends. It is often ordered as a snack or as a filler item where rice or noodle dishes are the main course.

Oyster Omelette is rather oily, which calls for a stomach-cleansing cup of Chinese tea.

58

POPIAH
P-OH-PEE-AH

A sort of spring roll, this meal-in-a-wrap is often eaten as a side dish, a snack, or as food for sharing among friends. The skin is paper-thin and made of wheat flour. The filling comprises bangkwang (Chinese sweet white turnip) that is peeled, cut into matchstick strips and then braised till soft and sweet. Bits of cooked tofu, pork meat, shrimp, bean sprouts and strips of omelette are placed atop the bangkwang, while a cool lettuce leaf, spread with a sweet sauce (either a dark sweet soya sauce, or a combination of shrimp paste and soya sauces) and chilli sauce, enfolds all the ingredients. Depending on the hawker, other ingredients may include slices of lapcheong (waxed Chinese sausage), shredded coriander leaves, chopped peanuts and fried shallots.

As Popiah is prepared fresh after you order it, you can almost always request for certain ingredients to be omitted, e.g., shrimp or chilli sauce. The hawker will typically wrap all the ingredients then slice the Popiah into four or five pieces. To be truly authentic, remember to eat your Popiah with your chopsticks.

* You may also like Kueh Pie Tee.

59

PORRIDGE

Chinese emperors ate porridge when feeling under the weather. You might feel like eating it everyday after tasting this comfort food. There are three main types of porridge in Singapore – the Cantonese version comprises rice that is boiled into a smooth, almost paste-like consistency, called congee, or jook. The Hokkien version is coarser in texture. Both versions are served with your choice of duck, fish, chicken, beef, minced pork, peanuts or century egg. The third version of porridge in Singapore is Teochew Porridge.

If you are feeling adventurous, look out for Raw Fish Porridge or Frog Porridge. Though not as common, these dishes are delightful local favourites.

Porridge is usually eaten hot and with You Tiao (see page 191).

You may also like Teochew Porridge.

60

PRAWN DUMPLING NOODLES

There's nothing dumb about eating these meat dumplings. In fact, they look pretty smart at the centre of this dish – the filling is a mixture of minced pork, water chestnut, and shrimp, all of which are seasoned with soya sauce, salt and pepper. The dumpling skin is smooth and thin. When cooked, the skin becomes translucent, allowing you to almost make out the filling, including the bright red shrimp meat, inside.

The juicy meat dumplings are served with thin yellow noodles, similar to angel-hair spaghetti, called mee kia, or flat yellow noodles, similar to fettuccine, called mee pok. The dish is served either dry or with soup. You can also order just Prawn Dumpling Soup, without noodles. Such a soup dish often accompanies other main dishes, like Chicken Rice. Prawn dumplings are considered the fatter brothers of wantons, which are dumplings stuffed with mainly minced pork.

* You may also like Wanton Noodles.

61

PRAWN NOODLES

The noodles will win you over. Then the soup will bowl you over. A delicious shrimp or seafood stock is made by frying the shrimp, and sometimes other seafood, with onions and garlic, and then immersing the shrimp in water and boiling them till all the lovely shrimp flavour emerges. Sometimes, pork bones are also added to enhance the soup with a sweet meaty flavour.

Thick yellow egg noodles, called mee, are served in the soup which is topped with large freshly cooked shrimp, fried shallots and coriander. Foodies will go ga-ga over the amazingly tasty and satisfying soup, while some hawkers may spoil their customers by serving up large juicy jumbo shrimp with the dish.

Prawn Noodles, also called Hae Mee, is not to be confused with Hokkien Mee. While Hokkien Mee is braised noodles in a semi-thick gravy, Prawn Noodles is most definitely a soupy dish, with the mouth-watering seafood soup making or breaking the dish. You can also order this dish dry, with the soup served in a separate bowl.

ROAST DUCK RICE

This is roast duck, Cantonese style, at its chopsticks-licking best. Expect shiny, reddish-brown crispy skin embracing succulent, juicy meat. Choice pieces of scrumptious duck are served over rice and topped with a thick brown meaty gravy that binds all the flavours together.

It is common to order Roast Duck to share with friends. The hawker will often also sell Char Siew. Ordering these roast meats is often a mouth-watering experience, especially for those hearty meat-eaters among us!

Cantonese Roast Duck is not to be confused with another duck rice dish, called Duck Rice, Teochew Duck Rice or Boneless Duck Rice. This is a braised duck rice dish, whereas Cantonese Roast Duck is unabashedly and extravagantly oily, crispy roasted game meat at its best!

Cantonese Roast Duck can also be served with noodles, usually mee kia, which are thin yellow noodles, similar to angel-hair spaghetti.

You may also like Char Siew Rice.

ROTI JOHN
ROW-TEE JOHN

Think French toast with a whole lot more happening on top. For instance, a spicy minced mutton paste is mixed with raw eggs and the combined mixture spread onto slices of baguette and then fried on a hot griddle. The result is a savoury and hearty French toast-type meal named Roti John because it used to be the favourite snack of the ubiquitous British "Johns", those British servicemen that were stationed in Singapore during the colonial times.

Enjoy this local favourite with a frothy Teh Tarik (frothy tea).

* *You may also like Chapati, Roti Prata and Murtabak.*

64

ROTI PRATA
RO-TEE PRAH-TAH

While the Italians conquer the world with their pizzas, the Indians have flipped up an ace of their own: Roti Prata, also known as Prata. Roti Prata is an unleavened bread, like pita, that is fried till crisp and golden. It is served with curry and eaten with fork and spoon. Something similar to the Roti Prata is the Murtabak, but the latter tends to be bigger and the fillings are more traditional, usually meat or vegetables. In contrast, the Roti Prata, though smaller, has taken on a creative slant as hawkers have started adding interesting fillings including ice cream, banana, cheese, egg and mushroom. In addition, there are now various types of Roti Prata in Singapore. Regular Prata is crispy, yet fairly thick, like a pita. Then there is Crispy Prata which is deliciously more crispy than the former, and thinner too. Thirdly, there is Paper Prata – a parchment-thin Prata that is almost thinner than a crepe. Finally, there is Coin Prata which is the size of a coaster or smaller. Try it as you won't be short-changed.

You may also like Chapati, Murtabak and Roti John.

SINGAPORE CLASSIC

153

65

SAMBAL STINGRAY
SAHM-BALL STINGRAY

This dish should fly with those who like barbecued fish. Stingray wings have tender mild flesh with no bones, only cartilage. This makes it perfect for grilling in this classic Singapore style – slathered in a fragrant rempah, wrapped in a banana leaf and barbecued over charcoal. Although usually a spicy dish, a non-spicy version can usually be prepared for you, upon request.

Barbecued Sambal Stingray is usually served on a banana leaf with a scoop of sambal chilli and a slice of cut lime on the side. The style of wrapping food in a banana leaf and barbecuing it over charcoal is often applied to fish fillets, sotong (squid) and shrimp as well.

* *You may also like Otah.*

66

SATAY
SAH-TAY

Sort of like mini-kebabs, but with just meat, no veggies. Small chunks of meat are marinated in spices like turmeric, cumin, fennel, lemon grass, old ginger and sugar, then skewered on bamboo sticks and barbecued over an open charcoal fire. The turmeric gives the meat its characteristic slightly yellowish tinge.

Satay is served with spicy peanut sauce, chunks of onions and cucumbers, and ketupat (compressed rice cakes) that are cooked in individual baskets of woven coconut leaves. It is usually eaten as a snack or as food for sharing.

Satay is served at both Malay and Chinese stalls. At the former, your choice of meat will be chicken, mutton and beef (Muslims do not eat pork). At the latter, chicken, mutton and pork will be offered (Buddhists and Hindus do not eat beef).

67

SATAY BEE HOON
SAH-TAY BEE-WHON

Nonpareil in other parts of the world is a plate of cooked rice vermicelli, garnished with freshly cooked ingredients – such as sliced shrimp, cockles, cuttlefish and tofu – and then summarily doused with a large scoop of the most amazing peanut gravy.

Rich, spicy, sweet and nutty, the peanut gravy is the star of this dish and is what separates the ordinary from the truly stellar versions. The gravy is made from freshly ground peanuts, curry powder, tamarind and water. It should not be too watery, but often covers the entire dish in a thick sultry brown layer that tempts you to stick your chopsticks in to explore what lies beneath.

The cockles are sometimes semi-cooked as cooked ones taste rubbery. Then again, the choice is yours.

68

SAYUR LODEH
SAH-YAH LOW-DAY

Don't like vegetables? Why not? Vegetables are only bland when you allow them to be. No chance of that happening for Sayur Lodeh. This Malay dish is a non-spicy creamy coconut vegetable stew that typically contains long beans, cauliflower, carrots, turnips and tofu chunks. Sometimes, eggplant and baby corn are also added for more texture and crunch. If you order Nasi Padang, this dish is a must as it balances the more substantial meaty dishes.

You will not have any problem finding a hawker that sells Sayur Lodeh, Beef Rendang and Chicken Curry. Just head straight for the Nasi Padang stall with its sumptuous display of homecooked dishes.

* You may also like Beef Rendang, Chicken Curry and Tauhu Telur.

69

SLICED FISH NOODLE SOUP

The Cantonese claim it – they call it Yu Tow Mai Fun. Foodies literally queue up for it (at some stalls, sometimes up to an hour). And most would agree that it's tough choosing between the pearly-white steamed fish slices and the fried fish fillets (seasoned and deep-fried until golden brown and crispy). How wonderful if you could have the best of both worlds, you ask. Actually, you can. You can even ask for evaporated milk to be added to the soup for a fuller, creamier stomach-soothing experience. Ginger slices ensure the dish is never fishy but always peachy.

Sliced Fish Noodle Soup can be served with a variety of noodles – bee hoon (rice vermicelli), chor bee hoon (thick rice vermicelli), mee kia (thin yellow noodles, similar to angel-hair spaghetti) or mee pok (flat yellow noodles, similar to fettuccine).

***You may also like Crab Tang Hoon or Fish Bee Hoon.**

70

SOON KUEH
SOON KU-AY

A popular breakfast food, this ivory or off-white dumpling is shaped in a semi-circle, just like the Curry Puff. However, unlike the Curry Puff, it is not deep-fried, but steamed. The skin is made from rice flour and is usually smooth and translucent. Depending on the thickness of the skin, you could sometimes just about make out the fillings inside, which comprise strips of bangkwang (Chinese sweet white turnip) cooked to a moist tenderness, dried shrimp, carrots and black mushrooms.

Soon Kueh is often served with chilli and dark soya sauce (thick and slightly sweet). White, red and black: the rather stark palette belies a palate-pleasing flavour blending savory, sweet and spicy. Soon Kueh is a popular snack at any time of the day.

* You may also like Ang Ku Kueh, Char Siew Bao, Chee Cheong Fun, Chwee Kueh and Muah Chee.

71

SOTO AYAM
SOH-TOE AH-YAHM

Better than chicken soup for the soul is spicy chicken soup for the soul. This soup dish originated in Indonesia, and has a characteristic yellow chicken broth that gets its colour from turmeric. The soup is seasoned with ginger, garlic, galangal, coriander, cumin and lemon grass. Coconut milk is added for additional fragrance and creaminess. Soto Ayam is served with rice.

Another version of this dish is Mee Soto – where thick yellow noodles, called mee, are soaked in the same soupy concoction and topped with shredded chicken, sliced cabbage, bean sprouts and slices of boiled eggs and potato cakes.

* You may also like Mee Rebus.

72

SOUP KAMBING
SOUP KAHM-BING

A close cousin of oxtail soup: that is one way to relate to this dish. To be more precise, Soup Kambing is a spicy mutton soup of Indian-Muslim origin. Bite-sized mutton chunks are removed from the bone and braised in curry powder and spices like cinnamon, cardamom and fennel till extra tender.

Visually, the thick broth is a potent-looking greenish-brown colour, but the rich aroma of spices and the lack of a strong mutton smell usually whets the appetite sufficiently. Hawkers often add a generous dose of pepper and fresh coriander leaves to the dish. Slices of soft baguette are used to soak up the broth.

* You may also like Soup Tulang.

73

SOUP TULANG
SOUP TOO-LANG

If you are a sucker for the exotic, this dish should thrill you to the bone. In essence an Indian-Muslim mutton soup, the delight of this dish is sucking the marrow out of stewed mutton bones, a pleasure indescribable to the uninitiated.

Soup Tulang comprises mutton leg or shoulder bones covered in a thick, gravy broth of curry powder and spices like cinnamon, cardamom and fennel. To extract the marrow, you can try sucking it out by placing your mouth at the entrance of the bone. Alternatively, tap the bone and if you're lucky, the marrow will slip out unbroken. Although the marrow may look slug-like, it has a melt-in-your-mouth texture which some have compared to foie gras. The rest of the mutton – involving delicious tendons and soft meat – is also wonderful.

Often, bright red colouring is added to Soup Tulang, giving the dish a startling blood-red appearance. Soup Tulang is often served with baguette.

✱ *You may also like Soup Kambing.*

SOYA SAUCE CHICKEN NOODLES

Glistening with promise, slices of tender chicken with luscious brown skin (from being braised in soya sauce for a long time) are placed atop the yellow noodles, similar to angel-hair spaghetti, called mee kia. The entire dish is moistened with brown stock and served with green leafy vegetables. You can also ask for mee pok (flat yellow noodles, similar to fettuccine). Whatever your choice, serious satisfaction is usually the outcome.

To maximise your enjoyment of Soya Sauce Chicken Noodles, venture to add a little chilli paste to the dish. It makes the noodles ever so piquant in the sense that they lightly sear the tongue. When it comes to food, flavour favours the bold. All said, it's rather foolhardy to pile on the chilli without a glass of cool drink!

75

TAUHU GORENG
TAO-WHO GO-RING

Crisp on the outside, tender on the inside. This is a tofu salad with a distinctive spicy, salty, sour and sweet sauce. Once you place your order of Tauhu Goreng, a slab of tofu is taken and deep-fried till brown and crispy. It is then sliced into 4 or 6 chunks. The insides, however, remain tantalisingly soft and creamy. They are served on a bed of boiled bean sprouts. A unique sauce made from tamarind, dark soya sauce, ground peanuts, chilli and palm sugar is drizzled on top. Sometimes, fermented black beans are also added to the mixture.

Tauhu Goreng is sold at Nasi Padang stalls, together with other classic Malay dishes like Beef Rendang, Chicken Curry, Sayur Lodeh and Tauhu Telur.

✻ You may also like Tauhu Telur.

76

TAUHU TELUR
TAO-WHO TEH-LURE

Put a couple of modest ingredients together adroitly and you'll be surprised how they rise to the occasion. The sublime combination of egg and tofu is deep-fried till crisp before dark, sweet soya sauce is added and topped with shredded cucumber and carrots, ground peanuts, sliced onions and bean sprouts. What makes Tauhu Telur unique, being much more than tofu omelette, is the fact that it is usually prepared in the shape of a tall tower. The egg and tofu mixture is fried in a small rounded mould, enabling layers of tofu and egg to be "stacked" on top of each other, to create a lovely crispy fragrant mountain of yummy goodness. Expect the tallest dish on the table to make a statuesque impact.

Tauhu Telur is available at Nasi Padang stalls. A sizeable dish, Tauhu Telur is usually shared between two and three persons.

* You may also like Beef Rendang, Chicken Curry, Sayur Lodeh and Tauhu Goreng.

77

TEOCHEW PORRIDGE
TEE-OOH CHEW PORRIDGE

Unlike Cantonese-style and Hokkien-style porridge, which is thick and smooth, Teochew Porridge, also known as Teochew Mui, is watery and grainy. It is served with an assortment of side dishes, which you can choose – fish cake (slices of fish paste), braised chicken feet, braised pork belly, steamed egg, braised cabbage, fried egg, ngoh hiang (deep-fried pork spring rolls) and braised eggplant in thick soya-based gravy are just some of the many dishes available for you to choose.

Typically, Teochew Porridge is shared among friends, so that more side dishes can be ordered for everybody to try. It is not uncommon for people to order two bowls of porridge per person, since the porridge is quite light. Locals like to quench their thirst with a bowl of porridge water, called Um, which is nutritious, clean tasting and free of charge.

* You may also like Porridge.

78

THOSAI
TOH-SAY

Order. Sit. Anticipate. Usually made fresh on the spot, the key characteristic of Thosai is its slightly fermented taste – it is a crispy, savoury crepe made of lightly fermented rice flour and dhal (lentils). This popular South Indian dish is cooked on a griddle and the Thosai is often folded into a roll, before being served hot and brown with chutney. There's plain Thosai and masala Thosai, which is filled with non-spicy curried mashed potatoes. Thosai is eaten with fork and spoon. Usually.

Eating Thosai using your bare hand (as the local Indians and Malays are wont to do) intensifies the experience, what with the tactile interaction with the food. It is polite to use only the right hand to handle your food, and only the first three digits of your hand. (Use the right thumb to shovel the morsels into your mouth.) Hawker centres and food courts in Singapore are equipped with toilets and washing basins.

79

THUNDER TEA RICE

An overcast sky comes to mind when you think about this exquisitely healthy spread that is mostly vegetables. Thunder Tea Rice, also known as Lei Cha Fan, gives you a choice of white rice or brown rice. It is topped with an array of condiments, including ikan bilis (dried anchovies), groundnuts, coriander, Chinese parsley, dried shrimp, chai poh (dried preserved radish bits) and diced portions of cabbage, pan-fried tofu and long beans. Accompanying the rice and condiments is a bright green bowl of "tea" whose appearance often induces surprise. This "tea" is actually made from an Asian pesto of ground green tea leaves, basil, mint, coriander and Chinese parsley. The pesto is added to water to create a refreshingly light and minty soup that is meant to be added to the rice.

This is one of those combinations that "work", notwithstanding the significant health benefits the dish is purported to bring, including slimming, aiding constipation, combating flu and lowering cholesterol. What more can a health-conscious foodie ask for?

You may also like Yong Tau Foo.

VEGETARIAN COOKED FOOD

As its moniker suggests, this hawker stall serves purely vegetarian options, but do not be fooled into thinking that vegetarian food is necessarily tasteless, colourless and uninspiring. In fact, vegetarian dishes, like vegetarian char siew (roast pork), mock fish and duck (all made from gluten), braised cabbage and sliced braised pumpkin and mushrooms, often taste as if they were cooked with an extra dose of oil to boost their flavour. Not surprisingly, they're usually quite toothsome. To allay the oily sensation, simply sip on a cup of Chinese tea, available at every coffeeshop.

Vegetarian dishes are often served with rice or bee hoon (rice vermicelli). All said, vegetarian cooked food is healthy and extremely affordable (unless you go to a posh vegetarian restaurant), typically costing less than $4.00 per hearty meal. Good for the heart and wallet.

81

WANTON MEE
WAN-TAHN MEE

The Chinese love their dumplings, and this dish is a big reason why. Juicy pork meat dumplings wrapped in silky translucent skin are the highlights of this dish. These dumplings, called wantons, are served with mee kia, which are thin yellow noodles, similar to angel-hair spaghetti.

There are two versions of this dish – the "dry" version comprises dumplings that have been deep-fried to a sizzling crisp. Soup is served on the side. The "soup" version sees the dumplings boiled, for the more health-conscious. Foodies will often judge Wanton Mee by the springy nature of the noodles which should not stick or clump together, and the freshness of the wantons. Some hawkers pride themselves on making the noodles of this dish themselves, instead of buying ready-made noodles from factories. The noodles from such hawkers are more often than not springy and tasty.

* *You may also like Prawn Dumpling Noodles.*

82

YONG TAU FOO
YONG TAO FOO

If you are someone who can't make up your mind, stay away from this stall – there are too many goodies to choose from. The main ingredients here are tofu and vegetables stuffed with minced pork or fish paste. You are allowed to choose the ingredients you want (good luck if you find yourself in a queue behind someone indecisive), which may also include fish balls, mock crabsticks and cuttlefish. You will also be asked to choose the type of noodle you want – mee (thick yellow noodles), mee kia (thin yellow noodles, like angel-hair spaghetti), bee hoon (rice vermicelli) or even, kway teow (white flat rice noodles).

Yong Tau Foo, also known as Niang Dou Foo, is served as either a soupy dish or dry, with a characteristic sweet sauce and sesame seeds. It is tasty, healthy (depending on your choice of ingredients), and very affordable. So pile it on.

* You may also like Thunder Tea Rice.

83

YOU TIAO
YOU TEE-AWH

Believe it or not, You Tiao dates back thousands of years to the story of Yue Fei during the Southern Song dynasty. Today, every Chinese loves this unwieldy cleft cruller that crackles with every bite. Tall, thin, tantalising and ever-tasty, the savoury snack is made from flour, yeast, baking soda, butter and water.

Often eaten at breakfast, You Tiao (sometimes called Yu Char Kueh) goes perfectly with Porridge, hot coffee or Tau Huay (see page 225) and a momentary disregard for calorie count.

* *You may also like Curry Puff and Goreng Pisang.*

DRINKS AND DESSERTS A TO Z

Chinese

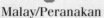

Malay/Peranakan

Indian

You'll be amazed to find such a wide variety of drinks and desserts available at the humble food court and hawker centre. There are drinks to cool you down or to take away that "oily" feeling in your stomach after chowing down on some all-too-artery-clogging fried dish. And there are hot and cold desserts – hot desserts provide that heartwarming feeling on a cold, rainy day while cold desserts perk you up on a hot, humid day.

Remember, if you cannot find the dish in this main section, look for it in **The Extremely Useful Index** at the back of the book. Sometimes, dishes are called by different names, but the index lists all the common names for all the dishes.

84

AH BOLING
AH BOWL-LING

These little ivory-white glutinous rice balls are filled with red bean, green bean, yam, peanut or sesame seed paste, and served in a warm syrupy clear soup. Order Ah Boling when you crave for a warm, sweet comfort dessert. Innovative hawkers have begun to add unique fillings to the rice balls, including durian! The syrupy clear soup is also sometimes replaced with soya bean milk. In any case, Ah Boling is a fairly healthy dessert that won't make you regret the additional calories.

And should you fall in love with these mushy confections, you can buy them at supermarkets in Singapore (at the frozen produce section). They're precooked, and you just have them to reheat the dumplings in the convenience of your home, hotel room or serviced apartment.

85

BUBOR CHA CHA
BOH-BOH CHA CHA

You don't need a sweet tooth to enjoy this "beady" concoction, though it helps. A good old-fashioned dessert that can be served either hot or cold, Bubor Cha Cha comprises soft sweet beads of cooked sweet potato and yam, together with slightly chewy sago pearls or cubes of sago (sago is from the sago palm tree, which looks like a typical palm tree). The ingredients are held together by sweetened coconut milk which is usually fragranced by pandan leaf and topped with gula melaka (palm sugar).

Gula melaka is prized for its caramel and butterscotch undertones. Do remember to stir your Bubor Cha Cha thoroughly as gula melaka is very sticky. It's a favourite sweetener for confections because gula melaka gives desserts that satisfying edge that mere sugar and brown sugar cannot. Go for Bubor Cha Cha and let your taste buds dance!

86

BUBOR TERIGU
BOH-BOH TE-REE-GOO

This is the "white version" of its hugely popular cousin: Pulut Hitam. A wholewheat dessert, Bubor Terigu, also known as Pulut Terigu ("terigu" means "wheat" in Indonesian), comprises white wheat beans that are boiled to a porridge consistency, flavoured with pandan leaf and gula melaka (palm sugar). Gula melaka is used instead of white sugar as the former gives this dish a better aroma. Coconut milk is trickled on top to add visual appeal.

The wheat beans, which look like barley, are cooked to just the right crackling softness. If they are undercooked, they will be too hard, and they will have no bite if overcooked. The hawker may ask you if you would like coconut milk, which adds a creamy sweetness. Mix well before eating. This dish is best enjoyed warm, so let it cool a bit before digging in.

✻ You may also like Pulut Hitam.

87

CHENDOL
CHEN-DOLE

Not something you would find in most Western cultures, this sweet cold dessert's signature ingredients consist of tiny, bright green jellied strips of bean flour immersed in sweetened coconut milk that has a slight pandan flavour. Other ingredients typically include shaved ice, boiled red beans, creamed corn, brown syrup, chewy attap chee (palm seeds) and jelly. Chendol can be served in a bowl or a tall mug/cup.

A popular dish that originated from Java, Indonesia, there are several versions of Chendol in Singapore, reflecting our local and cosmopolitan tastes. You may be keen to try Durian Chendol, which includes a dollop of durian puree or syrup to the mix. Or, for a more westernised version, go for Chendol with ice cream.

✶ You may also like Ice Kachang.

88

CHENG TNG
CHENG-TEHNG

A light dessert that can be ordered hot or cold, Cheng Tng comprises a sweet clear soup made primarily from longan and rock sugar. Ingredients like herbal jelly, barley, white fungus and Chinese dates are added to the soup. In addition, special ingredients like slices of dried persimmon, candied winter melon, sweet potato chunks and gingko nuts are sometimes added, depending on the hawker.

Cheng Tng is a local favourite that is ordered warm on a cold day to warm up the body, and taken cold on a hot day to cool you down. The cold version comes with crushed ice. Hot Cheng Tng tends to be sweeter since there is no ice diluting the soup. As the dessert is soup-based, you can order Cheng Tng at hawker centres and food courts to quench your thirst without relying on canned drinks.

89

CHIN CHOW

Chin Chow jelly is a black jelly that is made from boiling the Chinese herb leaf, called Chin Chow, that is part of the mint family. Also known as grass jelly, Chin Chow is made into a drink by adding syrup and water. It can also be served as a dessert – a bowl of chilled Chin Chow cubes is served with lychee or longan to make a refreshing treat on a hot day.

This dessert complements a heavy meal of rich food because of its light and palate-cleansing taste. It may come in a tall glass or a bowl depending on where you order it. The glass version has Chin Chow strips so you can greedily suck them up through a straw. The bowl version features bigger-piece or spaghetti-like Chin Chow that you can eat with a soup spoon.

* You may also like Ice Jelly.

90

ICE JELLY

A simple crushed-ice dessert featuring not-too-sweet jelly topped with fruit cocktail and served with sliced lime. What an avalanche of refreshment!

These days, innovative hawkers have begun to add all sorts of new ingredients to this refreshing dessert. You may find Ice Jelly served with soursop puree – soursop is a local fruit that is sour-sweet in taste – or sea coconut, a chewy fruit also known as coco de mer. Other innovations include the addition of lychee, another local fruit, mango puree or even, strawberry puree. The variations are almost endless and all very lovely.

Like Chin Chow, this dessert complements a heavy meal of rich food because of its light and palate-cleansing taste. On its own, Ice Jelly is thoroughly enjoyable and it doesn't fill you up.

91

ICE KACHANG
ICE KAH-CHANG

When asked to name a local favourite dessert, most Singaporeans would chorus "Ice Kachang!" This bowl of shaved ice shaped like a mountain is famous for its brightly-coloured appearance, thanks to the colourful sweet syrups that dress up the ice. Evaporated milk and sweet corn are drizzled on top for further colour and flavour.

It is a local favourite past time to "dig for treasure" in Ice Kachang. Underneath the mounds of fluffy shaved ice lie "hidden treats" which can be found using your spoon – like red beans, green beans, green chendol strips, jelly and at least one attap chee (palm seed). Innovative hawkers have started serving Ice Kachang with creative dressings like durian puree, mango puree, chocolate syrup, ice cream and fruit cocktail. In addition, there are two traditional forms of Ice Kachang worth highlighting – Peanut Ice Kachang comes with a swoon-worthy topping of freshly roasted ground peanuts while Gula Melaka Ice Kachang eschews bright colours, using only brown-black gula melaka (palm syrup), a sweet thick syrup, to colour the ice mountain.

✳ You may also like Chin Chow.

92

KOPI/TEH
KOH-PEE/TAY

These universal beverages come in many beguiling guises. Understanding the subtleties lets you customise your coffee or tea to suit every mood and weather. (In local lingo, Kopi means coffee, while Teh is tea.)

Kopi/Teh C: With evaporated milk and sugar.

Kopi/Teh C Kosong: With evaporated milk but without sugar.

Kopi/Teh Kar Tai: With condensed milk, and more sugar.

Kopi/Teh Kosong: Without sugar or milk.

Kopi/Teh Kow: Strong brew.

Kopi/Teh O: Without condensed milk, but with sugar.

Kopi/Teh Peng: Iced coffee/tea with condensed milk and sugar.

Kopi/Teh Poh: Light coffee/tea.

Kopi/Teh Siew Tai: With condensed milk, but less sugar.

Teh Tarik: "Pulled" tea with a frothy top. (see Teh Tarik entry for more details).

Teh Halia: Tea with ginger water.

Teh Masala: Tea with Indian masala spices.

93

LIME JUICE

Think of pick-me-ups and one naturally thinks of caffeine. Well, this non-caffeinated drink is so bracingly sour, you will shudder with glee. Lime Juice is the perfect complement to normally oily (but oh so flavourful) hawker dishes like Chicken Rice, Hokkien Mee, Roast Duck Rice and Char Kway Teow. The juice, freshly squeezed from vitamin C-rich lime of the green variety, is a refreshing, cooling drink that is sweetened slightly with syrup or sugar. (Trust the citric acid to act powerfully against oily food.)

Don't be surprised to find sour plums inside your drink, which amplify the tart factor. Enjoy the citrus aroma and invigorating zest as you nurse an icy tall glass of this powerful quencher. Not recommended for those suffering from gastric pain.

✱ You may also like Plum Juice and Sugarcane Juice.

94

PLUM JUICE

Another lovable drink that helps you to feel cleansed and healthy after a bout of oily hawker food. Plum Juice is made from suan mei (preserved sour plum) and sweetened with sugar. It has a distinctive tart and sweet taste, but is less tart than Lime Juice. Plum Juice is usually served ice cold in balmy Singapore to enhance the refreshing experience. The hazel-coloured drink may contain one or two full-size dried plums to make it look more authentic and desirable.

Plums contain several antioxidants and are known for their laxative effect. This effect has been attributed to various compounds present in the fruits, such as dietary fibre. Plum Juice, like Lime Juice, is also rich in Vitamin C and could help regulate the functioning of the digestive system if drunk regularly.

* You may also like Lime Juice and Sugarcane Juice.

95

PULUT HITAM
POO-LOOT HEE-TAHM

Black glutinous rice is roasted to release its nutty flavour, then boiled to porridge consistency, flavoured with pandan leaf, cornstarch, sugar and gula melaka (palm sugar). Although black when uncooked, the rice turns dark purple or maroon when cooked in low heat until all the sugar dissolves. The result is a hot starchy dessert with a rather intense aroma and husky texture. The dessert is made creamier and more fragrant by drizzling coconut milk on top. (When you order Pulut Hitam, it's common for the vendor to enquire if you would like coconut milk.)

Pulut Hitam as a dessert is fairly filling. While it is usually served piping hot, let it cool a little as it tastes best when warm. Purplish canvas with a pearly swirl. Perfect.

* You may also like Bubor Terigu.

96

SAGO GULA MELAKA
SAY-GO GOO-LA MAH-LA-KA

This saccharine pudding is made from sago pearls (from the sago palm tree, which looks like a typical palm tree). Sago, a starch like tapioca, is extracted and produced commercially in the form of "pearls": little white balls the size of rice grains that turn translucent when boiled. The cooked sago pudding is doused in gula melaka (palm sugar) and topped off with rich thick coconut milk. The combination of smooth, springy pearls, sweet nutty-flavoured gula melaka and creamy fragrant coconut milk makes this local dessert a true delight for many locals.

The ingredients may be simple, but the taste will win you over. This dessert is especially good after a meal of barbecued seafood or roasted meats as it smooths out the oily aftertaste from the palate. Stir well to break up the sago clump and to dissolve the irresistible gula melaka.

97

SOYA BEAN MILK

If there is such a thing as milk without the lactic taste, this would be just the drink. Soya Bean Milk is made from soaking and straining softened soya beans and then adding water and rock sugar. An all-round beneficial and delicious beverage for the hot Singapore weather. Soya Bean Milk contains almost the same amount of protein (but not the same amino acid profile) as cow's milk, but with less fat. No wonder Soya Bean Milk is promoted as a healthy alternative to cow's milk for those sensitive to lactic acid.

These days, modern hawkers have created new soya bean drinks, including almond soya, wheatgerm soya, cocoa soya and grass jelly soya (soya bean milk with cubes or strips of black jelly added).

Equally good whether hot or cold (the hawker will ask for your preference when you order). A truly great-tasting mainstay in Singapore's hawker culture.

❋ You may also like Tau Huay.

SUGARCANE JUICE

Did you know that drinking Sugarcane Juice goes back 5,000 years in Chinese history? Today you can get freshly pressed Sugarcane Juice in Singapore hawker centres because hawkers bring in big sticks of freshly cut sugarcane and compress them using huge metal machine rollers at their stalls. Fresh Sugarcane Juice is mild, frothy, pale green and clean tasting. If you prefer, your mug of Sugarcane Juice will come with a small lime for a big kick; the hawker usually asks when you place your order.

This juice is as natural as it gets, and the sugar contained in the product does not turn into fat but leaves your body without creating any fat. It contains protein, iron, phosphorus, vitamins A, B1, B2, B3, and C, calcium, and chromium. A thirst quencher that turns other drinks green with envy.

* You may also like Lime Juice and Plum Juice.

SINGAPORE CLASSIC

99

TAU HUAY
TAO HWAY

Look at it and it glistens like liquid. Shake it and it wobbles. Eat it and it melts in your mouth and leaves nothing on the waistline. (Yes, it's common to see smartly coiffed lady executives bending over dainty bowls of Tau Huay in hawker centres.) A super soft tofu pudding (or beancurd custard) made of coagulated soya bean milk, Tau Huay is loved for its soft, silky texture sweetened by clear syrup. This tofu pudding can be ordered hot or cold. Definitely nutritious, non-fattening, cholesterol and guilt free.

The telltale sign of good Tau Huay is the smoothness and softness of the custard. It's probably the cheapest dessert with wow factor that you can buy. Nowadays you'll find Pandan Tau Huay, Almond Tau Huay and other innovative concoctions. Pay $2.00, and keep the change and your figure.

* *You may also like Soya Bean Milk.*

100

TAU SUAN
TAU SOO-AHN

This dessert is neither soup nor porridge, and it helps to think outside the box in order to enjoy it. It is one of the few desserts that Singaporeans eat – for breakfast! Tau Suan is split green bean (or mung bean without the skin) soup, served hot with slices of You Tiao (fried dough crullers) to infuse a slightly salty touch to an essentially sweet dessert. The beans are green when husked, but once shelled, they are sun-yellow, hence the die-die-must-try (local way of saying must-try) appearance of this dessert. They are soaked, steamed, and boiled with rock sugar, water and pandan leaf. The soup is slightly thickened with potato starch for a more filling gastronomic experience.

Though a Chinese dessert, Tau Suan is loved by just about everyone and you should not miss the opportunity to try it. It is good as a snack or as a dessert.

101

TEH TARIK

Foamy at the top but robust all round. This concoction is a mixture of black tea, condensed milk, and a good deal of skills without the spills. Literally meaning "pulled tea" in Malay, this hot tea beverage is prepared by the signature process of "pulling" the tea – to the distance of an arm's length – when pouring back and forth between two vessels. However, the process of "pulling" the tea is not practised in all stalls, simply because not everyone can do it! The greater the distance, the better the perceived taste. This process not only cools the tea, but also blends the condensed or evaporated milk nicely. That's why you seldom see a spoon served with Teh Tarik, as there's nothing to stir.

Usually Malay or Indian-Muslim owned, the stall that sells Teh Tarik typically sells food like Roti Prata and Nasi Biryani as well. But some, called "sarabat" (the term is less frequently used in modern Singapore) stalls, are known to sell only drinks.

THE ULTIMATE STREET FOOD TOURS

The way to a man's heart is through his stomach. And the way to the heart of Singapore… is through filling your stomach with Singapore's best street food! So follow these scrumptious Ultimate Street Food Tours and eat your way through classic Singapore dishes, discover the culinary genius of several distinct cultures (Chinese, Malay, Indian and Peranakan), and experience the ins and outs of Singapore's delightful local street culture.

The dishes recommended here are commonly found in all air-conditioned food courts, as well as the more "earthy" hawker centres. Let your stomach lead the way. Be adventurous – you'll kick yourself if you miss out!

SINGAPORE CLASSICS IN THREE DAYS

DAY 1

START HERE

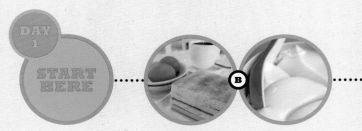

Start your day with the well-loved combination of Kaya Toast and Kopi, a typical breakfast for locals. The silky, warm flavours of Tau Huay complete the meal, leaving you energised for a day of exploration and adventure.

A must-try, Chicken Rice is an unforgettable Singapore street food classic.

Like Carrot Cake, Oyster Omelette is gritty street food at its fried-up aromatic best.

To cool down after all that heat, Ice Kachang and Sugarcane Juice are in order.

S

The classic pick-me-up,
Carrot Cake, will shock
your senses with its mix
of sweet, salty, crispy
and chewy.

D   **D**

Why not trot down to Lau Pa Sat Festival Market or
East Coast Lagoon Food Village and experience a classic
Singapore BBQ Seafood Dinner? Chilli Crab, Black Pepper
Crab, Sambal Stingray, Otah… don't forget to savour
a few sticks of Satay, which are authentically prepared
over smoky charcoal fires in the open air.

B Breakfast
L Lunch
D Dinner
S Snack

FOOD TOUR 1
SINGAPORE CLASSICS IN THREE DAYS

DAY 2

START HERE

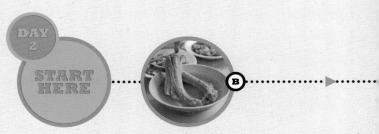

B

Head down to Chinatown Complex
Market for a hearty breakfast of
Bak Kut Teh, a feisty bowl of peppery
pork ribs served with rice.

L

S

Laksa is a classic dish that has
been known to bring street food lovers
to tears because of its spicy, out-of-
this-world taste. Or, order another
street food classic, Char Kway Teow,
and enjoy a perfect plate of moist,
savoury fried noodles.

Egg Tarts have a
rich buttery crust
and a wobbly fragile
egg-based centre.

D

Try some Chendol for a great
way to end your day!

Roti Prata makes a perfect snack! These flattened
fried doughs are served with curry or sugar. Or, try
Popiah and Kueh Pie Tee, Peranakan dishes that
you won't find in other parts of the world.

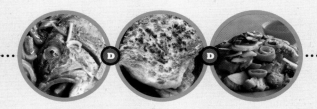

Another Singapore Classic Dinner is in store
– but this one requires Fear Factor-level courage.
Head down to Little India for some Curry Fish Head.
Pair this Indian classic with Murtabak,
Indian Rojak and Tiger Beer, for a thoroughly
adventurous local dinner.

B Breakfast
L Lunch
D Dinner
S Snack

SINGAPORE CLASSICS
IN THREE DAYS

DAY
3

START
HERE

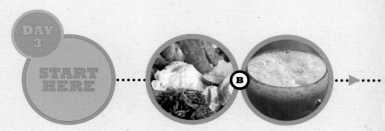

Treat yourself to a classic Malay
breakfast – fragrant Nasi Lemak, washed
down with Teh Tarik. Ah, heaven! Too much
cholesterol? Tell that to the locals happily
chomping away around you!

Hokkien Mee requires an expert hawker
hand to fry it till just right – not too mushy,
yet gooey enough to be slurpy. Simply out
of this world. Supplement with colourful,
crunchy Indian Rojak.

Reward yourself with the most savoury Chinese dinner
– Roast Duck Rice and Barbecue Chicken Wings, paired with
Prawn Dumpling Soup and Lime Juice. Mind-blowing!

This snack is admittedly
harder to find these days.
But if you do find it,
do not miss the chance
to order Chwee Kueh.

Plum Juice and Ice Jelly
are the perfect complements to
complete your heart-stirring,
stomach-satisfying lunch.

We guarantee you have
never tried anything like
Chinese Rojak – a salad
that is crunchy, sweet,
sour, salty, chewy, fruity
and oily all at once!

B Breakfast
L Lunch
D Dinner
S Snack

FOUR-IN-ONE:
THE ART OF SAVOURING FOUR
CULTURES PACKED IN ONE DAY

START HERE

Your multi-cultural adventure begins
with a breakfast of Roti Prata, Nasi Lemak
and Teh Tarik at Geylang Serai or Adam Road
Food Centre, to fully immerse yourself in
Indian and Malay culture.

Feast on Nasi Padang for lunch. Soak in Malay
culture by ordering Beef Rendang, Curry Chicken,
Sayur Lodeh, Tauhu Telur and Lontong.

Sink your teeth into delicious Peranakan
snacks, Popiah and Kueh Pie Tee,
to revive your tired body.

As a snack, nibble on the crispy fried Chinese dish of Carrot Cake to keep your energy up.

You'll be licking your lips and exclaiming, "Sedap!" at the end of the meal. ("Sedap" means delicious in Malay.)

For dinner, dig into some classic Chinese street food with Chicken Rice, Oyster Omelette, Cheng Tng and Lime Juice.

B Breakfast
L Lunch
D Dinner
S Snack

FOOD TOUR 3
NOODLES ADVENTURE

START HERE ⋯ **B** ⋯➤

For breakfast, dig into
Mee Goreng or Mee Siam, both
spicy Malay noodles dishes.

L

For lunch, treat yourself to a plate
of Char Kway Teow or Hokkien Mee.

D   **D**

Think noodles for dinner may not be filling enough?
You clearly have not tried Crab Tang Hoon.
But if you're looking for a light dinner, Hor Fun
or Ipoh Hor Fun might just do the trick.

Sample the popular Bee Hoon, a favourite breakfast choice for the young and old.

Or, try the simple, unpretentious yet brilliant-when-well-executed dishes of Bak Chor Mee or Wanton Mee.

B Breakfast
L Lunch
D Dinner

HEALTH IS WEALTH:
A GUILT-FREE DAY

START HERE

B

Healthy street food is not a misnomer.
For breakfast, savour interesting yet healthy
versions of Porridge, like Raw Rish Porridge,
Teochew Porridge or Frog Porridge.

L

For lunch, there is nothing quite as
palate-cleansing as Sliced Fish Noodle Soup.
Or, if you crave for rice, look out for
Thunder Tea Rice, a dish that will make
you feel healthier with every bite.

D

For dinner, feast on Yong Tau Foo, a noodle
dish that is served with lots of tofu-based
side dishes, vegetables and fish balls.
Reward yourself with a healthy dessert
of Tau Huay, made of soya beans.

For a toothsome snack, choose Popiah, as it is freshly made with few deep-fried ingredients.

Your mid-afternoon snack is the light dessert Cheng Tng or Chin Chow to help you cool down from the heat.

B Breakfast
L Lunch
D Dinner
S Snack

Breakfast	Lunch	Dinner

DAY 1

DAY 2

DAY 3

Breakfast	Lunch	Dinner

DAY 4

DAY 5

DAY 6

RECOMMENDED FOOD COURTS AND HAWKER CENTRES

"Be adventurous – take a combination of train, bus and taxi and be rewarded with a truly authentic hawker experience in the heartlands of Singapore!"

All major shopping centres in Singapore have food courts, air-conditioned food halls where people have a choice of at least 10 stalls to order various types of hawker food from. Food courts allow locals and tourists alike to enjoy delicious hawker food in air-conditioned sit-down comfort. The major food court chains are Food Junction, Food Republic, Kopitiam and Koufu.

Hawker centres are stand-alone buildings where a variety of hawker food is sold by several stalls. These buildings range from being 30 years old to being newly refurbished. All of them are not air-conditioned, though some have ceiling fans for ventilation. Some locals will swear by their favourite hawker centre, and insist that the hawker food at these places are more authentic and delicious than the food prepared in the sanitised upmarket environment of air-conditioned food courts. Hawker centres are generally harder to get to, because most of them are not in the city centre or tourist areas. Be adventurous – take a combination of train, bus and taxi and be rewarded with a truly authentic hawker experience in the heartlands of Singapore!

Generally speaking, food courts do not open for breakfast, but hawker centres do. For an authentic local breakfast, head down to a hawker centre in a local neighbourhood, or try out Killiney Kopitiam or Toast Box, two new chains of breakfast outlets which serve authentic local breakfast items in the air-conditioned comfort of shopping centres.

Orchard Road/Scotts Road/Somerset Road

313@Somerset – Food Republic

🚇 313 Orchard Road, Level 5
🕐 Monday – Sunday 10am – 10pm
🚉 Nearest MRT Station: Somerset MRT Station

Cathay Cineleisure Orchard – Koufu Food Court

🚇 8 Grange Road, #B1-01
🕐 Monday – Sunday 9am – 9pm
🚉 Nearest MRT Station: Somerset MRT Station

ION Orchard – Food Opera

🚇 2 Orchard Turn, #B4-03/04
🕐 Monday – Sunday 10am – 10pm
🚉 Nearest MRT Station: Orchard MRT Station

National Youth Park – Kopitiam

🚇 121 Somerset Road
🕐 Monday – Sunday 10am – 10pm
🚉 Nearest MRT Station: Somerset MRT Station

Newton Food Centre

🚇 500 Clemenceau Avenue North
🕐 Monday – Sunday 24 hours
🚉 Nearest MRT Station: Newton MRT Station

Plaza Singapura – Kopitiam

🚇 68 Orchard Road, #06-15
🕐 Monday – Sunday 10am – 10pm
🚉 Nearest MRT Station: Dhoby Ghaut MRT Station

Wisma Atria – Food Republic

🚇 435 Orchard Road, 04-00
🕐 Monday – Sunday 10am – 10pm
🚉 Nearest MRT Station: Orchard MRT Station

IN THE CITY
Specialising in Breakfast

313@Somerset – Toast Box   (AC)
- 313 Orchard Road, Level 5, Food Republic
- Monday – Sunday 8am – 10pm
- Nearest MRT Station: Somerset MRT Station

Centrepoint – Toast Box   (AC)
- 176 Orchard Road, #B1-02A
- Monday – Sunday 8am – 10pm
- Nearest MRT Station: Somerset MRT Station

Plaza Singapura – Toast Box   (AC)
- 68 Orchard Road, #01-23
- Monday – Sunday 8am – 10pm
- Nearest MRT Station: Dhoby Ghaut MRT Station

Wisma Atria – Toast Box   (AC)
- 435 Orchard Road, #B1-55/60
- Monday – Sunday 8am – 10pm
- Nearest MRT Station: Orchard MRT Station

Killiney Kopitiam   (AC)
- 67 Killiney Road
- Monday – Sunday 6am – 8pm
- Nearest MRT Station: Somerset MRT Station

Lucky Plaza – Killiney Kopitiam   (AC)
- 304 Orchard Road, #01-10
- Monday – Sunday 7am – 7pm
- Nearest MRT Station: Orchard MRT Station

Paradiz Centre – Killiney Kopitiam   (AC)
- 1 Selegie Road, #01-03
- Monday – Sunday 7am – 11pm
- Nearest MRT Station: Dhoby Ghaut MRT Station

Funan Digitalife Mall – Food Junction   (AC)

- 109 North Bridge Road, #05-24/34
  Monday – Sunday 11am – 10pm
- Nearest MRT Station: City Hall MRT Station
- North Bridge Road exit

Makansutra Gluttons Bay @ Esplanade   (❋)

- 8 Raffles Avenue, #01-15
- Monday – Sunday 6pm – 3am
- Nearest MRT Station: City Hall MRT Station,
  Esplanade exit

Millenia Walk – Koufu Food Court   (AC)

- 9 Raffles Boulevard, #02-02
- Monday – Sunday 9am – 9pm
- Nearest MRT Station: Promenade MRT Station,
  Suntec City exit

Plaza By The Park – Kopitiam   (AC)

- 51 Bras Basah Road, #01-03
- Monday – Sunday 10am – 10pm
- Nearest MRT Station: Bras Basah MRT Station
  North Bridge Road exit

Raffles City Shopping Centre – The Food Place   (AC)

- 252 North Bridge Road, #03-15/17
  Monday – Sunday 10am – 10pm
- Nearest MRT Station: City Hall MRT Station,
- Raffles City exit

Suntec Convention Centre – Food Republic   (AC)

- 1 Raffles Boulevard, Level 1
- Monday – Sunday 10am – 10pm
- Nearest MRT Station: Esplanade MRT Station,
  Suntec City exit

Marina Square – Killiney Kopitiam   (AC)
- 6 Raffles Boulevard, #02-230A/231A
- Monday – Sunday 7.30am – 8pm
- Nearest MRT Station: Esplanade MRT Station, Marina Square exit

---

Millenia Walk – Killiney Kopitiam   (AC)
- 9 Raffles Boulevard, #01-93/94
- Monday – Sunday 7.30am – 8pm
- Nearest MRT Station: City Hall MRT Station, Suntec City exit

---

Purvis Street – Killiney Kopitiam   (AC)
- 30 Purvis Street
- Monday – Sunday 7am – 8pm
- Nearest MRT Station: City Hall MRT Station, Raffles City exit

---

Bugis

Bugis Junction – Food Junction   (AC)
- 230 Victoria Street, Level 3, #03-03
- Monday – Sunday 11am – 10pm
- Nearest MRT Station: Bugis MRT Station

Raffles Hospital – Kopitiam   (AC)
- 585 North Bridge Road, #01-02/03/05/06
- Monday – Sunday 10am – 10pm
- Nearest MRT Station: Bugis MRT Station

VivoCity/Harbourfront/Sentosa

Harbourfront Centre – Food Junction   (AC)
- No. 1 Maritime Square, #03-01/04
- Monday – Sunday 10am – 10pm
- Nearest MRT Station: Harbourfront MRT Station

Seah Im Food Centre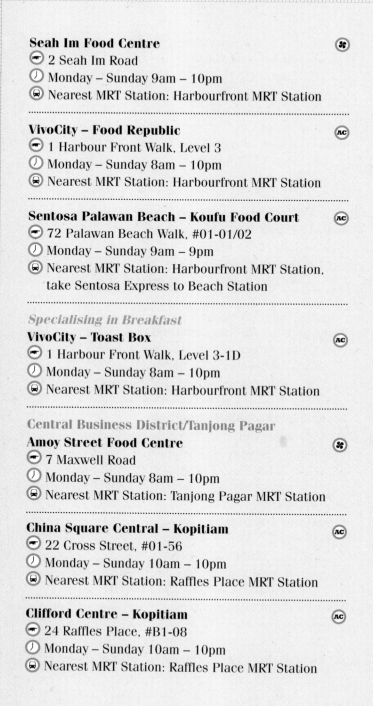
🚇 2 Seah Im Road
🕐 Monday – Sunday 9am – 10pm
🚌 Nearest MRT Station: Harbourfront MRT Station

VivoCity – Food Republic
🚇 1 Harbour Front Walk, Level 3
🕐 Monday – Sunday 8am – 10pm
🚌 Nearest MRT Station: Harbourfront MRT Station

Sentosa Palawan Beach – Koufu Food Court
🚇 72 Palawan Beach Walk, #01-01/02
🕐 Monday – Sunday 9am – 9pm
🚌 Nearest MRT Station: Harbourfront MRT Station, take Sentosa Express to Beach Station

Specialising in Breakfast

VivoCity – Toast Box
🚇 1 Harbour Front Walk, Level 3-1D
🕐 Monday – Sunday 8am – 10pm
🚌 Nearest MRT Station: Harbourfront MRT Station

Central Business District/Tanjong Pagar

Amoy Street Food Centre
🚇 7 Maxwell Road
🕐 Monday – Sunday 8am – 10pm
🚌 Nearest MRT Station: Tanjong Pagar MRT Station

China Square Central – Kopitiam
🚇 22 Cross Street, #01-56
🕐 Monday – Sunday 10am – 10pm
🚌 Nearest MRT Station: Raffles Place MRT Station

Clifford Centre – Kopitiam
🚇 24 Raffles Place, #B1-08
🕐 Monday – Sunday 10am – 10pm
🚌 Nearest MRT Station: Raffles Place MRT Station

Lau Pa Sat Festival Market ❀

- 18 Raffles Quay
- Monday – Sunday 10am – 10pm
- Nearest MRT Station: Raffles Place MRT Station

Market Street – Koufu Food Court (AC)

- 146 Market Street, #01-46
- Monday – Sunday 9am – 9pm
- Nearest MRT Station: Raffles Place MRT Station

Tanjong Pagar Plaza Food Centre ❀

- 6 Tanjong Pagar Plaza
- Monday – Sunday 7am – 8pm
- Nearest MRT Station: Tanjong Pagar MRT Station

Specialising in Breakfast

Amoy Street – Killiney Kopitiam (AC)

- 21 Amoy Street
- Monday – Sunday 7am – 8pm
- Nearest MRT Station: Tanjong Pagar MRT Station

Lorong Telok – Killiney Kopitiam (AC)

- 11 Lorong Telok
- Monday – Sunday 7am – 8pm
- Nearest MRT Station: Raffles Place MRT Station

IN CHINATOWN

Chinatown Complex Market ❀

- 335 Smith Street
- Monday – Sunday 7am – 8pm
- Nearest MRT Station: Chinatown MRT Station

Maxwell Road Food Centre ❀

- 1 Kadayanallur Street
- Monday – Sunday 8am – 10pm
- Nearest MRT Station: Chinatown MRT Station

People's Park Complex Food Centre ❄

🚐 32 New Market Road
🕐 Monday – Sunday 8am – 8pm
🚌 Nearest MRT Station: Chinatown MRT Station

The Central – Kopitiam (AC)

🚐 6 Eu Tong Sen Street, #04-86/91
🕐 Monday – Sunday 10am – 10pm
🚌 Nearest MRT Station: Chinatown MRT Station

IN KAMPONG GLAM

Geylang Serai Market and Food Centre ❄

🚐 1 Geylang Serai
🕐 Monday – Sunday 10am – 10pm
🚌 Nearest MRT Station: Eunos MRT Station

Golden Mile Food Centre ❄

🚐 505 Beach Road
🕐 Monday – Sunday 11am – 9pm
🚌 Nearest MRT Station: Lavender MRT Station

IN LITTLE INDIA

The Banana Leaf Apolo (AC)

🚐 54-58 Race Course Road
🕐 Monday – Sunday 10.30am – 10.30pm
🚌 Nearest MRT Station: Little India MRT Station

The Banana Leaf Apolo (AC)

🚐 48 Serangoon Road
🕐 Monday – Sunday 7am – 10.30pm
🚌 Nearest MRT Station: Little India MRT Station

Tekka Market ❄

🚐 665 Buffalo Road
🕐 Monday – Sunday 9am – 9pm
🚌 Nearest MRT Station: Little India MRT Station

IN LITTLE INDIA *(cont'd)*

City Square Mall – Kopitiam (AC)

- 180 Kitchener Road, #04-31
- Monday – Sunday 10am – 10pm
- Nearest MRT Station: Farrer Park MRT Station

AT THE AIRPORT

Changi Airport – Kopi @ T3 (AC)

- 65 Airport Boulevard, Basement 2 Mall
- Monday – Sunday 24 hours
- Nearest MRT Station: Changi Airport MRT Station

IN LOCAL NEIGHBOURHOODS

ABC Brickworks Food Centre (❋)

- Block 6, Jalan Bukit Merah
- Monday – Sunday 9am – 9pm
- Nearest MRT Station: Redhill MRT Station, and take a taxi

Adam Road Food Centre (❋)

- 2 Adam Road
- Monday – Sunday 7am – 9pm
- Nearest MRT Station: Newton MRT Station, and take a taxi

Changi Village Hawker Centre (❋)

- 3 Changi Village Road
- Monday – Sunday 7am – 9pm
- Nearest MRT Station: Tanah Merah MRT Station or Tampines MRT Station, and take a taxi

Chomp Chomp Food Centre (❋)

- 20 Kensington Park Road
- Monday – Sunday 7am – Midnight
- Nearest MRT Station: Serangoon MRT Station or Kovan MRT Station, and take a taxi

East Coast Lagoon Food Village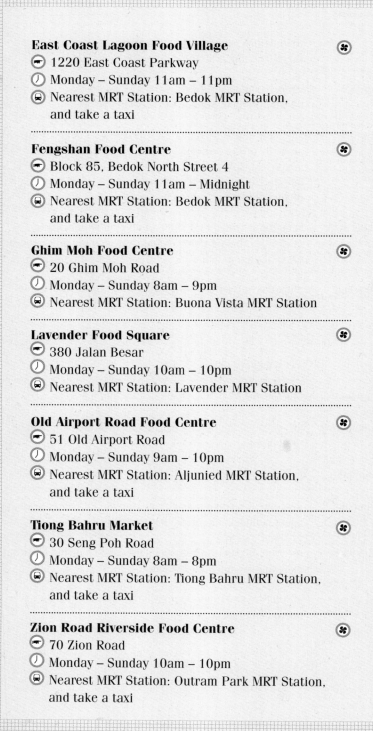

- 1220 East Coast Parkway
- Monday – Sunday 11am – 11pm
- Nearest MRT Station: Bedok MRT Station, and take a taxi

Fengshan Food Centre

- Block 85, Bedok North Street 4
- Monday – Sunday 11am – Midnight
- Nearest MRT Station: Bedok MRT Station, and take a taxi

Ghim Moh Food Centre

- 20 Ghim Moh Road
- Monday – Sunday 8am – 9pm
- Nearest MRT Station: Buona Vista MRT Station

Lavender Food Square

- 380 Jalan Besar
- Monday – Sunday 10am – 10pm
- Nearest MRT Station: Lavender MRT Station

Old Airport Road Food Centre

- 51 Old Airport Road
- Monday – Sunday 9am – 10pm
- Nearest MRT Station: Aljunied MRT Station, and take a taxi

Tiong Bahru Market

- 30 Seng Poh Road
- Monday – Sunday 8am – 8pm
- Nearest MRT Station: Tiong Bahru MRT Station, and take a taxi

Zion Road Riverside Food Centre

- 70 Zion Road
- Monday – Sunday 10am – 10pm
- Nearest MRT Station: Outram Park MRT Station, and take a taxi

Glossary

dry:
: when a dish is served dry, it means that the soup is served in a separate bowl from the main dish.

soup:
: when a dish is served with soup, it means that the soup is added into the main bowl of ingredients.

century egg:
: known as Pidan in Mandarin, this Chinese delicacy is made by preserving duck, chicken or quail eggs in a mixture of clay, ash, salt, lime, and rice hulls for several months. As a result, the yolk turns dark green and smells of ammonia for a taste to remember.

chilli padi:
: sometimes called bird chilli, chilli padi is the smallest of all chillies. Bright red in colour, it is also the hottest form of chilli there is.

dim sum:
: a type of Chinese meal involving a wide variety of small dishes, similar to Spanish tapas. The dishes are usually steamed or deep-fried, and are eaten for breakfast, lunch or tea.

dry fry:
: to fry without oil over low heat.

galangal:
: blue ginger.

Hokkien:
: a Chinese dialect group originating from Fujian province in China.

rempah:
: pounded spice paste.

sambal:
: a hot spicy paste made of a mixture of chilli and prawn paste pounded and blended together.

tamarind:
: the fruit of this tropical tree is used as a souring agent in many Indian and Malay dishes.

Teochew:
: a Chinese dialect group originating from Chaozhou province in China.

The Extremely Useful Index

First edition
Copyright © Epigram Pte Ltd, 2010

Published by
Epigram Books
1008 Toa Payoh North #03-08
Singapore 318996
Tel: (65) 6292 4456
enquiry@epigram.com.sg
www.epigram.com.sg

10 9 8 7 6 5 4 3 2 1

Distributed by
MarketAsia Distributors
601 Sims Drive #04-05 Pan-I Complex
Singapore 387382
Tel: (65) 6744 8483
jl@marketasia.com.sg

Written by
Ruth Wan and Roger Hiew

Main photography © Dr Leslie Tay

Additional photography by
Caslyn Ong (pp 2, 6, 7, 8, 14, 56, 66, 74, 78, 100, 122, 210)
Michelle Koh (pp 20, 21, 68)
Nicholas Leong (p 24)

Living Gallery picture (p 10)
Courtesy of the National Museum of Singapore

Supported by

National Library Board Singapore
Cataloguing-In-Publication Data
Wan, Ruth, 1976-
There's No Carrot in Carrot Cake/Ruth Wan, Roger Hiew.
Singapore: Epigram Books, 2010.
p. cm.
Includes index.
ISBN-13 : 978-981-08-2865-3 (pbk.)

1. Peddlers – Singapore – Guidebooks.
2. Roadside restaurants – Singapore – Guidebooks.
3. Singapore – Guidebooks. I. Hiew, Roger, 1966- II. Title.

TX907.5
647.955957 – dc22   OCN538153593

Printed in Singapore.
All rights reserved. No part of this publication may be reproduced or transmitted
in any form or by any means, electronic or mechanical, including photocopying,
recording or by any information storage and retrieval system, without the written
permission of the publisher.